Dr. Schulze's
5-Day
BOWEL
Detox

Dr. Schulze's
OFFICIAL PUBLICATIONS
Since 1979

Published by
Natural Healing Publications
P.O. Box 9459, Marina del Rey, CA 90292
1-877-TEACH-ME (832-2463)

Library of Congress Catalog
Card Number: Pending
**Create Powerful Health Naturally
with Dr. Schulze's 5-Day BOWEL Detox**
ISBN: 0-9761842-3-0

Dr. Schulze's 5-Day BOWEL Detox

WARNING

This book is published under the First Amendment of the United States Constitution, which grants the right to discuss openly and freely all matters of public concern and to express viewpoints no matter how controversial or unaccepted they may be. However, medical groups and pharmaceutical companies have finally infiltrated and violated our sacred constitution. Therefore, we are forced to give you the following WARNINGS:

If you are ill or have been diagnosed with any disease, please consult a medical doctor before attempting any natural healing program. Many foods, herbs or other natural substances can occasionally have dangerous allergic reactions or side effects in some people. People have even died from allergic reactions to peanuts and strawberries.

Any one of the programs in this book could be potentially dangerous, even lethal. Especially, if you are seriously ill.

Therefore, any natural method you learn about in this book may cause harm, instead of the benefit you seek. ASK YOUR DOCTOR FIRST, but remember that the vast majority of doctors have no education in Natural Healing methods and Herbal Medicine. They will probably discourage you from trying any of the programs.

"Never underestimate
the Power of Colon
Cleansing!"
— *Dr. Richard Schulze*

TABLE OF CONTENTS

"You can heal yourself of ANYTHING. ANY disease. ANY illness. Your body knows exactly how to create perfect health and heal you. All you have to do is STOP doing what makes you sick and START doing what will assist your body in healing itself. Then, the Miracle happens. Tomorrow is what you Believe and Do Today."
— *Dr. Richard Schulze*

FOREWORD
BY DR. RICHARD SCHULZE

Any sick and diseased person who seeks out cures from medical doctors, drugs and hospitals is attempting to buy the appearance of health, not earn true health.

MODERN MEDICINE
DISEASE COVER-UP AND HEALING ILLUSION

So-called "Medical" cures are actually illusions that may give the false appearance of health but they are actually cover-ups, band-aids, crutches and make-up. Neither the patient nor their doctor are correcting the real cause of their disease.

Instead, the doctor and patient come up with a treatment plan, usually the swallowing of very powerful chemical pills, that will relieve symptoms, chemically alter your metabolism and maybe even kill the disease.

Although this often appears to be a cure, the underlying cause of the illness (or what made them sick in the first place) was not addressed. The patient was not asked to change the faults in their lifestyle that created the disease initially. Since the cause of the disease was not dealt with or eliminated, the sickness continues to grow and flourish within them, often unnoticed at first, underneath this medically induced illusion of health. But eventually, sooner or later, it resurfaces with a vengeance.

A perfect example of this is the way medical doctors currently treat cancer. . . attempting to cut, burn and poison the cancer out of your body, but never addressing or correcting why you got it in the first place. This is why the horrifying medical statistics state that, after cancer treatment, the chances are your cancer will return in less than five years.

One of a thousand other examples of this medical illusion is that no one who takes insulin for diabetes is curing and healing their pancreas. In fact, just the opposite. As they become addicted to that drug their pancreas gets sicker, rots and eventually dies. The same is true for EVERY pharmaceutical drug made. Drugs chemically alter organs, cells and the normal function of your body to make it appear to run normally when it is actually still very sick. Often, drugs are used to allow you to continue to hurt yourself and make yourself sick. This is obviously apparent from the ads: eat anything you want and still enjoy mamma's cooking without indigestion, just swallow a few pills. While this deception is going on, you appear to be healthy while all the time your sickness grows, gets worse and eventually kills you.

Why do people do this to themselves? Why has this system of medicine flourished? It is quite simple. Most people that walked into my clinic were just like numb, dazed drug addicts when it came to how they lived their lives. They were addicted chemically, physically, emotionally and spiritually to everything from sugar, fast food, coffee and alcohol to sitting on their ass watching television that reinforced their unbalanced, insecure, mundane, dysfunctional, angry, fearful and diseased existence. The average American is following a feverishly paced destruction of their body, mind and spirit, numbing and killing themselves at every opportunity. The average American is the perfect stooge to Corporate America's gigantic junk food industry. The Average American is the perfect junkie to America's multi-trillion dollar drug and medicine business. The Average American is drugged, stoned, hypnotized, mesmerized, paralyzed and addicted to the American way of life, more precisely, to the American way of disease, drugs and death.

So, the average patients who walked into my clinic didn't want to change; they resisted it, hated it, were afraid of it... and only when numerous attempts at medical treatment eventually failed them, and only when they were in such pain that the drugs could no longer squelch it, and only when they were told that death was imminent, and only when their fear of disease, pain and death would become so strong that it would override their fear of change, would they drag themselves begrudgingly into my clinic door. After all, who would voluntarily inflict on themselves the horrifying depravation and torture that most people think is necessary to heal disease naturally and build lasting health.

For the elite of my patients, the professional disease masters who burnt the candle at both ends, lived life in the fast lane, partied hearty and had committed a continuous barrage of self-inflicted lifestyle beatings and assaults on themselves for 20, 30 or 40 years, at first it seemed sure that my frightening suggestions of fruit juices, raw vegetable salads and whole grains instead of cheeseburgers, french fries and milkshakes would certainly kill them. But very soon, they started feeling the power of health, energy and vitality which far exceeded the short-lived rush of sugar, caffeine, alcohol, cocaine and fast food. Soon, they started feeling the rush of nutrient-rich and clean blood circulating to their brain, which far surpassed any chemical-induced rush. Soon, even the most debauched of my patients became as addicted to health as they were to disease and a whole new wonderful world began to open up for them.

NATURAL HEALING
TRUE HEALING THAT CREATES POWERFUL AND LASTING HEALTH

By far most of my patients' biggest shock was the fact that the horrors that they expected from me and my programs really didn't exist. In fact, the product that I sold most in my clinic was simply COMMON SENSE!

Most of my patients were so shocked at how truly easy it was to change and live a new healthy life. Even the few who had a tougher time giving up the "good life" soon became so addicted to feeling good and having so much energy, that they immediately recognized their old ways as the true poisons that they were.

After a few visits, my patients began to see that the real torture was not inside my clinic, but outside my clinic. Because when your body is sick, it is simply because of what you are doing to yourself. You are sick because how you live is killing you. It's that simple. To cover up disease medically and just create the illusion of health takes very concentrated chemical drugs that have debilitating side effects. Often, this isn't enough, so people undergo mutilating surgical cutting and burning and all sorts of painful, horrifying, ghastly and expensive medical torture.

But inside my clinic, there was no cutting and burning, and no ghastly, horrifying and horrendous side effects. There was only health and healing.

Inside my clinic, my patients' pain was relieved and their diseases were cured, but not with drugs. Instead, I used my two basic fundamentals of healing disease and building health with Natural Healing.

STOP what you are doing that is making you sick.

START what cleans, nourishes, strengthens and heals your body.

I am smart enough to know that this divine, incredible and complex body that we are blessed with is far beyond my comprehension and understanding. I wouldn't ever try and bullshit anyone that I understand even 10% of what is going on inside all of us. And I certainly wouldn't expect you to believe that I knew enough

to go inside you, surgically or chemically, and heal disease. On the other hand...

Our bodies have many organs, numerous systems, thousands of chemicals and billions of cells that are designed to heal us of anything, and they will do this immediately, if we just give them the chance, the opportunity. And the way we give our body a fighting chance to heal itself is simply to create a healthy lifestyle, a healing environment, and our body will take over and do everything else that is needed.

How do I know this? Because for the last 30 years, I have instructed my patients, students and other doctors, all over the world, on how to create this healing lifestyle. How to live life in such a way that your body will heal itself and disease and sickness will literally leap out of your body.

What I know is how to live our lives in such a way that our bodies will heal themselves of ANY and ALL diseases known to mankind.

THE RESULTS: Over a hundred thousand patients have healed their diseases without medical doctors, drugs and hospitals, using only Natural Healing, Herbal Medicine and Good Common Sense.

"He [the patient] is looking to get something for nothing, not knowing that the highest price we ever pay for anything is to have it given to us. Instead of accepting salvation, it is better to deserve it. Instead of buying, begging or stealing a cure, it is better to stop building disease. Disease is of man's own building and one worse thing than the stupidity of buying a cure is to remain so ignorant as to believe in cures."
— Dr. John Tilden

DEDICATION
MY NATURAL HEALING MASTERS, TEACHERS AND PATIENTS

This book is dedicated first to the teachers of my great teachers: Henry Lindlahr, John Tilden, John Harvey Kellogg, Benedict Lust, Edward Shook, Jethro Kloss, Father Sebastian Kneipp, Randolph Stone and many others… many who followed the old German Nature Cure school of thought.

To my great teachers, especially Paavo Airolla, Dr. Bernard Jensen and Dr. John Ray Christopher, who all taught me the miraculous healing power of good thorough colon cleansing that healed thousands of patients in their clinics.

And finally, to my thousands and thousands of patients, who walked, crawled and were carried into my clinic over a span of 3 decades and put their trust in me. To the few who died and the many who survived and thrived, you were the ones who taught me what doesn't work, and more importantly, what does. And most importantly, what it takes to heal killer and life-threatening diseases and create powerful and lasting energy, vitality and health.

You are the ones who really taught me the miraculous healing power of colon cleansing.

COLON CLEANSING
TRAINING AND EXPERIENCE

As you can see from my dedication, I have the best training. If you want to heal yourself of disease and illness, and do it naturally, I am your man. But more importantly, I have experience.

While my friends were rocking and rolling to the sounds of the 60s, I spent the second half of my teenage years just trying not to die. Because I inherited a heart deformity from my parents, the top medical doctors said I would be dead by 20. Well, today I am happy to say that those medical doctors are all dead and that I am very much alive.

In my own personal healing journey, I experimented with bowel cleansing far beyond what I have ever seen published by anyone. I knew that in order for my body not to die, but instead to heal itself and build me a new heart, that I needed to be clean down to a cellular level.

Once I healed myself and went to school to study Natural Healing and Herbal Medicine, and worked in the clinics of my great teachers, I immediately saw the power of colon cleansing on a much bigger scale. At Dr. Bernard Jensen's clinic, I witnessed some of the most unbelievable sizes and shapes of fecal impactions that you could imagine streaming out of the patients. As Dr. Jensen himself on a daily basis would remind me, a dirty bowel was literally the root of all evil, the major cause of almost every disease.

Training under Dr. John Ray Christopher, an hour didn't go by when he wasn't exclaiming that to get a patient well I needed to get to the cause, behind the cause, behind the cause, behind the cause. In other words, he too knew that autointoxication from an impacted and malfunctioning intestinal tract was again the cause behind most diseases.

Years later in my own clinic, I soon discovered that even my teachers' programs were not effective enough because, in the heyday of their clinics, medical statistics say that only 10% to 30% of Americans had bowel disease and fast food was hardly even heard of. But in the prime of my clinical practice, there was now a fast food joint on every one of the four corners of every major city intersection and the medical books were now saying (in the 1980s) that about 50% of Americans have bowel disease and by the 1990s that 100% of Americans will have bowel disease as they grow old. Also the incidence of colon-rectal disease and colon-rectal cancer was skyrocketing, killing and infecting hundreds of thousands of Americans. So I had to take my great teachers' Natural Healing Routines and Herbal Formulae and crank the intensity, WAY UP!

As you'll see in this book, what my great teachers saw as their worst cases of constipation and colon disease were now the commonplace in my clinic. My great teachers would not have been able to imagine the far worse constipation and bowel disease that I would encounter just in the first few years of my clinical practice.

COLON CLEANSING
JUST NOT "COOL" ANYMORE

Today, we live in a much more politically correct time when most Natural Healing and herbal books are written by university professors and supposedly hip medical doctors. Even the few remaining true herbal authors are pathetically scrambling to be recognized, legitimized and licensed, so they can become real doctors of some sort. They have all shed and buried their natural roots, traded in their mortar and pestle for a stethoscope and a white jacket, ignored their sense of smell, taste and common sense for a data printout from a HPLC (High Performance Liquid Chromatograph) and denied their roots of the great herbalists of the past and would spit on their graves if it meant they could get recognized.

Consequently, they have thrown out many of the basic fundamentals of healthy living, especially colon cleansing, and just talk about the marker chemicals or standardization of herbal products and attend their bullshit association meetings and political gatherings. In the meantime, while they are sweeping colon cleansing neatly under the carpet for cleaner and more scientific things to talk about.

Americans are being diagnosed by the hundreds of thousands with more colon-rectal disease and colon-rectal cancer than EVER before in history!

Most herbalists and supposed herbal authorities today never ran a clinic, nor ever had any patients. If they had, they would know that colon cleansing should be at the top of their list of health programs, not being eliminated as old fashioned, dirty and uncomfortable to talk about.

Sure, I too wanted to be a cool, recognized herbalist when I first opened my clinic. I, too, wanted to heal the diseases of mankind, especially the life-threatening ones and the ones that medical doctors say are incurable or at best manageable, but can never be healed, and I too wanted to heal these people and their diseases with my secret formulae made from rare and exotic herbs from deep in the rainforest or high on the top of the Himalayas. BUT, I also knew that I first had to correct the FUNDAMENTAL things in life that my patients had screwed up, like their food program, their circulation and exercise and, of course, their constipation.

Well, my patients screwed me out of that dream. I always say that my patients had the nerve, the gall, to get better before I was ready for that to happen. They cheated me out of my fantasy about healing killer diseases with exotic herbs.

I thank God that what my great teachers knew, what they taught me and what I soon discovered, is that the fundamentals of good living HEAL ALL BY THEMSELVES. I didn't need all the fancy, smanchy stuff. I could see all my fantasies of joining my colleagues at their prestigious herbal associations quickly fading away.

In fact, 80% of my patients were healed after JUST doing my 5-Day BOWEL Detox.

What turned out to be my greatest clinical discovery is that my patients, suffering with EVERY KNOWN DISEASE, got well, healed, totally healed, almost EVERY SINGLE ONE OF THEM, and more importantly stayed disease-free and healthy for years, by just following the fundamentals of good healthy living and doing a thorough, complete colon cleanse.

Find this hard to believe? So did I. But my healed patients were sitting in my office with all of their medical tests, blood work-ups, ultrasound pictures, x-rays, biopsy reports and their poor prognosis, that said they were sick and dying... and now they had new medical tests, reports and pictures and very shocked medical doctors that couldn't exactly explain what happened. But sure enough, their disease was gone, vanished, and they were healed. Many of my patients were told by top medical doctors and oncologists that they would be dead in a few days, and they are still alive today, 20 years later. And their diseases, cancers, tumors, whatever, just went away. The proof was sitting in my office right in front of me. It was undeniable. Healing miracles do actually happen, and happened every single day in my clinic.

I DID THINGS A LITTLE DIFFERENTLY.

Now, I have to admit that my programs weren't exactly run of the mill. I am famous for being a hardass with tough programs. See, I figured early on that I had nothing to lose. My patients had already tried medical treatment and it failed them. Many were sent home to die, so big deal if I screwed up, they were dead anyway. For many of these patients Natural Healing and Herbal Medicine had failed them, also. Many told me that herbs and natural stuff just doesn't work. At first, I was very angry at their remarks and then I realized, THEY WERE RIGHT! Because when I looked around me at the current state of Natural Healing and Herbal Therapy, it was pathetic, real wimpy at best.

At least, the medical doctors knew how to deal with your disease with INTENSITY. My God, if you go to a medical doctor with a malignant cancer, well, they are going to cut, carve, gouge, rip and burn this cancer right out of your body. They will carve half of your face off or scoop a big chunk of your brain out, if necessary. If you die, heck, the disease was going to kill you anyway. They will burn your ass off with radiation, implant radium seeds into your lungs or ovaries and inject highly concentrated, extremely toxic, cell-killing chemicals directly into your bloodstream, while my colleagues were lighting candles, singing positive affirmations, and doing biofeedback.

What utter wimpy bullshit. The doctors knew that to heal raging killer diseases you had to sharpen your drills and saws, crank up and concentrate that radiation beam and boil down that chemo a little stronger, again while the Natural Healers were pussyfooting around with aromatherapy.

So in my clinic, I pulled out all of the stops and cranked up Natural Healing and Herbal Medicine all the way. I tried to kill my patients with hot and cold showers, drown them with water and juices and develop intensive programs that would either kill them or cure them. But I couldn't kill any of them; they just got better.

The same was true for the colon cleansing routines and herbal formulae of the era: they were weak. Many were antiques, hundreds of years old, when people got way more exercise and ate lots more unprocessed food. When I used these colon cleansing formulae in my clinic, my patients wouldn't even get a good fart, let alone a good bowel movement. So, I was forced to turn up the intensity. I created stronger and more powerful bowel cleansing programs and herbal formulae, far beyond anything that was available, until I started to get the job done, until my patients were getting their bowels cleansed and working again, until my patients were getting well. For some of my patients, I had to move out of human strength bowel cleansing herbs and research old veterinary books to find herbs that were stronger, that were actually used to clean the bowels of animals 10 times heavier than humans, like horses. It wasn't until I developed formulae with this kind of strength that my patients started getting healed.

As news spread of my aggressive and powerful Colon Cleansing, my colleagues and even some of my closest friends told me that I was going too far, that I would hurt people. Because the majority of them didn't

have clinics and never worked with patients, I guess they didn't realize what a bunch of tough, seasoned, hardass and constipated people Americans are, who are hell-bent on killing themselves living the "good life."

"Did you ever notice that when we are partying that it's full steam ahead? We have our foot on the gas pedal and we floor it. I have never heard of anyone, ever, that when drinking beer said, 'You know, Bob, we have each had a six pack of beer. Why do you think it is packed in sixes? Do you think we should call the beer manufacturer and see if having a seventh beer is an overdose?' Or did you ever hear of anyone that stopped eating after one bag of potato chips, one candy bar, a packet of cookies or two cupcakes, because they had already eaten the suggested adult serving? Hell no, we just pop open the seventh beer and the second bag of chips with absolutely no hesitation.

But... when healing ourselves and doing the best healthy thing that we have ever done for ourselves in years, we immediately take our foot off of the gas pedal and slam on the brakes. WHY? I have heard every silly and ridiculous question from 'can too much organic food hurt you' to 'can I overdose on Echinacea', but no one ever called me up and asked me if too much whiskey or pot was an overdose. I would tell my patients that if they would use half the energy and passion that they had used partying and killing themselves in their new health program, the disease would leap out of their body and they would be well tomorrow."

THE BOTTOM LINE... PUN INTENDED.

So with my **5-Day BOWEL Detox,** which frightened and scared my colleagues, I saw 80% of my patients have the majority of their symptoms disappear AND their sickness and disease retreat and disappear. Just by cleansing their colon as I suggested. What terrified other herbalists and natural doctors didn't scare my patients a bit. It just healed them.

Today, most people think that the extremely fast pace of modern life makes it inconvenient for them to take an extra two minutes out of their busy lives, a few times a day, to empty their body's waste from the largest organ in their body.

Today, the average person's high animal food diet containing ZERO fiber, combined with overprocessed and refined food that becomes an impacted, immovable toxic disease-causing sludge in their colon, makes it impossible for them to have normal bowel movements, even if they make the time.

Well, do I have the answer, and it is in this book with more straight medical facts and personal clinical experiences than you will see in print today.

In this book, you will clearly see that the real cause behind the majority of sickness and disease in America is the retention and storage of toxic, poisonous waste in our colon and the infrequency of its being emptied. In this book, I will show you how cleansing your colon will make the biggest healing difference in your life, help you to heal any disease and sickness and create powerful lasting health and vitality. Most importantly, I'll show you how to do it!

Dr. Richard Schulze

This book is dedicated to my son, Arthur, and all of our children. Let's teach them how to create healthy and strong bodies and open, flexible minds. This will ensure us all a future of PEACE, LOVE AND BLISS.

YOUR COLON

A basic understanding of how it works could save your life!

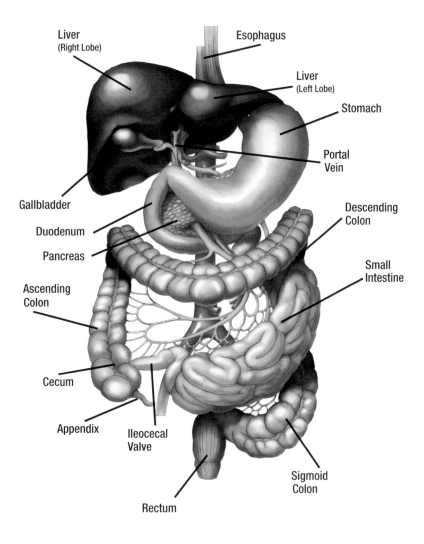

DIGESTIVE, ASSIMILATION & ELIMINATION TRACT

CHAPTER ONE
BOWEL ANATOMY AND PHYSIOLOGY 101

From your mouth to your anus, this intestinal tube is as long as two cars parked end-to-end.

30 feet

*Knowing what goes on in the last 5 feet of it can **Save YOUR LIFE!***

Thousands of patients walked into my clinic with stomach aches, but when I would ask them where their stomach hurt, they would almost always point to their colon instead, about 12 inches below their stomach! We walk around in our body for a 100 years, but have little or no idea where our particular organs are. Well, not anymore. In this chapter, I will show you where your digestive system and colon are and put an end to the mystery.

Your colon is the last stage of your digestive tract and has many jobs. Having a basic understanding of your colon's functions can keep you healthy and prevent disease.

THE 30-FOOT LONG JOURNEY

I will take the liberty here of actually describing the entire digestive and elimination tract. The main reason for this is I don't know the next time I will get close to this subject and it may be helpful to many of you to understand the upper gastrointestinal anatomy and physiology. And as always, if this section is more than you can comprehend, drop it. There will be no test, and you can heal yourself of anything without knowing the following information. Saying that...

THE DIGESTIVE AND ELIMINATION TRACT

The digestive and elimination tract is one long tube from your mouth to your anus, just shy of 30 feet long. There is only one way in and one way out. This tube is often referred to as the alimentary canal or tract, which includes the mouth, esophagus, stomach, duodenum, small intestine, large intestine, rectum and anus.

THE ESOPHAGUS

In your mouth, when you chew, saliva is produced from the salivary glands and mixed with food. This is often referred to as the first stage of digestion, because saliva enzymes initiate the digestion of starches. Saliva also lubricates the food for its initial travel down the esophagus. The esophagus is about 9 inches long and takes swallowed food down to your stomach. Where the **ESOPHAGUS** meets the stomach, there is an **esophageal sphincter muscle,** which relaxes to let food enter the **stomach** and then contracts to prevent the backup of stomach contents.

THE STOMACH

The **STOMACH** is a muscular sac with a mucosa lining. This lining secretes gastric juices, like hydrochloric acid and pepsin, that help to further digest your food. These juices begin the digestion of proteins. Just the sight and smell of food triggers the excretion of gastric juices. Bad habits like chewing gum continually stimulate and fool the stomach into thinking food is on the way and can lead to digestive and stomach trouble. Also, animal foods, especially beef and pork, are almost impossible to digest and require the constant secretion of acid, which can lead to stomach and duodenal ulcers, burnt tissue and eventually holes in your stomach and intestinal lining. (*OK, I know I strayed to Natural Healing and not anatomy and physiology.*)

At the end of the stomach is the **pyloric valve**, which keeps the stomach's contents in the stomach until they are sufficiently processed and digested to move on. This valve and the emptying of the stomach's contents is triggered by hormones, nerves and other factors.

THE SMALL INTESTINE

As food is released from the stomach through the pyloric valve it enters the duodenum, which is technically considered the first part of the small intestine. The **duodenum** is almost a foot long. When partially digested food, sometimes referred to as **chyme**, enters the duodenum, it triggers the release of hormones. These **digestive** hormones are released from the walls of the duodenum and stimulate the **liver** and **gallbladder** to release **bile,** which enters the duodenum through the **common bile duct**. These hormones also stimulate the **pancreas** to release **pancreatic juices** into the duodenum through the same common bile duct, sometimes referred to as the pancreatic duct. These liver and pancreatic juices continue the process from the stomach, breaking down carbohydrates and proteins. But now, these juices also start to break down fats. The walls of the duodenum secrete digestive juices, too.

The second part of the small intestine, which is about 9 feet long, is called the **jejunum**. The third and last part of the small intestine is called the **ileum**. It is 13 feet long and terminates at the **ileocecal valve** at the beginning of the colon or large intestine. The wall of the entire small intestine, all three parts, are folded and look like accordion pleats. These folds have even smaller folds on their surface small projections called **villi,** about 3/8ths of an inch

long. There are even **micro-villi** that are smaller. Obviously all of these folds increase the surface area of the small intestine. Since this is where the majority of food absorption takes place, the more surface area to absorb, the better. Each **villus** (the singular of villi) contains a capillary network which introduces the digested food nutrients into your bloodstream. The **portal vein** transports this digested food first to your liver and then, if deemed acceptable, onward into your entire circulatory system to feed every cell in your body.

THE LARGE INTESTINE

At the end of the small intestine is the ileocecal valve, which allows food to pass into the large intestine, colon or bowel, whatever you want to call it. The large intestine (see illustration on page 18) is about 5 feet long and 7 inches in circumference. It has no villi, but still can absorb water, vitamins and minerals from the intestinal contents. This process dries the intestinal contents and turns them into waste (fecal matter) for release or defecation.

The first part of the large intestine is called the **cecum**. The **vermiform appendix**, about 3 to 4 inches long, is right below the illeocecal valve. It is an immune system aggregation similar to the tonsils, adenoids and the Peyer's patches in the small intestine. Here is the perfect placement to detect any pathogen or micro-organism that may be harmful to you as the digested food enters the final stage of digestion ready for elimination. This is also the biggest anti-gravity and uphill trek for the food. The vermiform appendix also excretes fluids that lubricate the food and stimulate peristalsis, the muscular contractions of the colon that move the food and eventually fecal matter along. The parts of the large intestine are referred to in order: **cecum, ascending colon, hepatic flexure (the first turn near the liver), transverse colon, spleenic flexure** (downward bend near the spleen), **descending colon, sigmoid colon, rectum** and **anus**. Parasites are often found in the cecum and in the appendix. It is their favorite breeding ground and hiding place. Constipation, on the other hand, is most often found in the descending and sigmoid colon. The rectum is about 5 inches long and is considered the end of the colon. The anus is the sphincter muscle at the end of the rectum that opens to release the undigested and unassimilated food residue called feces, fecal matter, stool or excrement. I don't know who was the first person to take a good look at and examine feces—probably a guy like me—but in any case, examination of the stool is a diagnostic art in itself. Color, form, consistency, odor and the presence of blood, mucous and parasites can all tell a story about a patient's health and have been used by doctors for centuries to diagnose disease. Medical doctors today still use a stool sample to detect colon cancer and many other diseases.

"My FIRST RULE with all of my patients was to get their bowel cleaned out. Then the healing begins."
— *Dr. Richard Schulze*

THE AVERAGE AMERICAN COLON

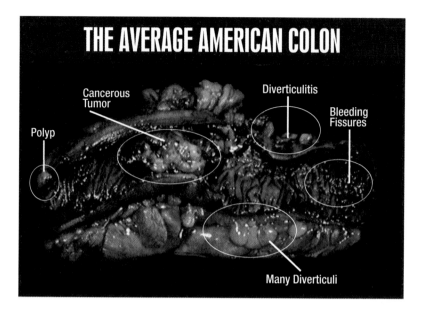

Polyp

Cancerous Tumor

Diverticulitis

Bleeding Fissures

Many Diverticuli

THE "PERFECT" COLON

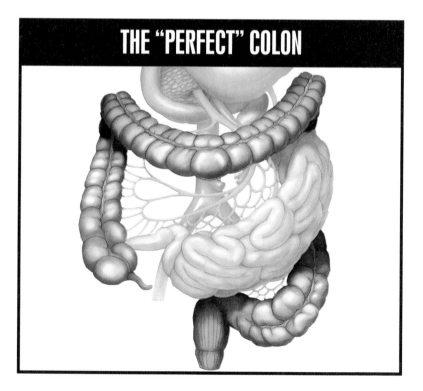

CHAPTER TWO
COLON DISEASE AND COLON CANCER

In their lifetime, the average American eats:

- 12 three thousand pound cows

- 6 whole pigs

- 3,000 chickens, turkeys and other flying birds

- 3,000 fish, sea creatures and sea scavengers

- 30,000 quarts of cow's milk

- 30,000 aspirin and pain killers

- 20,000 over-the-counter and prescription drugs

- 2,000 gallons of alcohol

Per year...

- 500 doughnuts

- 400 candy bars

- 300 soft drinks

- 170 pounds of white, refined sugar

WHAT CAUSES 100% OF AMERICANS TO END UP WITH COLON DISEASE?

- In the U.S., **we eat** more than **1,000,000 animals an hour.**

- Every day, **49% of ALL Americans** take one or more pharmaceutical drugs.

- In 1972, we spent 3 billion a year on **fast food**. Today, **we spend more than 110 billion.**

LOOK WHAT THEY PUT IN THEIR BODIES!

Just imagine all of that dead decaying flesh, junk food and drugs going into your mouth, all of it passing through your digestive tract into your bloodstream, your brain, your heart and then out through your liver, bowel and kidneys. This fiberless feast causes the average American to be **70,000 BOWEL MOVEMENTS SHORT** in their lifetime.

THE LATEST MEDICAL STATISTICS

What makes hot news isn't necessarily an accurate reflection of what is really going on in the world. This is especially true when it comes to what people are dying from.

Breast Cancer: Black tie galas are being held all over America to raise money for breast cancer research. October has been declared National Breast Cancer Awareness Month. The word "mammogram" is on every woman's lips, and if all that isn't enough I received an invitation to a black tie gala in New York, "Penthouse Pets Bare Their Breasts For Breast Cancer." I am NOT kidding.

Prostate Cancer: Every man is dreading his next prostate exam, while every magazine you pick up has an article on prostate cancer.

AIDS: Every day there is another article or something on the radio or television about AIDS. It has totally changed our lives, from how we have sex to police officers wearing rubber gloves.

And while all our attention is on breasts, the prostate, AIDS and sex... **colon cancer kills 400% more people than AIDS! It actually KILLS more men and women in America than breast cancer or prostate cancer.**

Yes, according to the Center for Disease Control (CDC), death from AIDS has declined significantly in the past 5 years. It's down a whopping 70%, but the AIDS media blitz still continues. SEX SELLS. Many reporters have told me that no one wants to hear about poop and that breasts, prostates and sexual diseases are more sexy and sex-related and, therefore, more newsworthy. But sexy or not, AIDS only kills about 15,000 Americans a year. Prostate cancer will kill about 39,000. Breast cancer will kill about 40,000. But, colon-rectal cancer will kill about 60,000 Americans this year with over 150,000 new cases diagnosed. I know, I've heard all the excuses: *"It's dirty, it's embarrassing, and I don't want to talk about poop."* Or my favorite: *"I'm too busy to be going to the bathroom all the time."* **Like ostriches with our heads buried in the sand, we don't want to discuss colon disease or health.**

Although colon-rectal cancer and disease is reported in most modernized countries, American's high levels of constipation and our unwillingness to talk about it has helped us win the international contest hands down. We have now awarded ourselves the highest incidence of colon cancer and disease of any country in the world. And according to medical statistics…

EVERY American will develop some type of colon disease, polyp, tumor or colon cancer in their lifetime. So it's high time we started talking about what's causing it, how to heal it, and more importantly, HOW TO PREVENT IT.

LET'S CHECK WHAT THE TOP MEDICAL DOCTORS SAY

The Merck Manual is written by the most distinguished and respected group of top medical doctors and pharmaceutical manufacturers in the world. It is the medical industry's standard text for the diagnosis and treatment of disease. **This book tells us that colon degeneration is on the rise.**

EVERY AMERICAN EVENTUALLY HAS DIVERTICULOSIS OR HAS MANY DIVERTICULA.

The incidence of diverticulosis (herniated bowel pockets caused by constipation) has increased dramatically over the past 50 years. It states that in 1950 only 10% of adults over the age of 45 had this disease; in 1955, 15%; in 1972, 30%; and in 1987, 45%. The most recent edition states that the incidence increases rapidly over age 40 and that **every person will have diverticulosis if they live long enough**. Diverticula are sac-like herniations through the muscular wall of the colon that are caused by increased pressure in the bowel from constipation. By old age, every American has many. They are filled with trapped fecal sludge, they

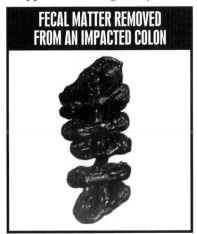

FECAL MATTER REMOVED FROM AN IMPACTED COLON

become infected and the rotting feces erodes the surrounding mucousa. Blood vessels rupture, then infection begins.

UP TO 50% OF AMERICANS HAVE POLYPS IN THEIR COLON!

A polyp is a tumor that arises from the bowel surface and protrudes into the inside of the colon. **Most polyps eventually transform into malignant cancer tumors.**

Alternative Healers, Natural Healers and the new breed of "HIP" medical doctor authors have all ignored the latest disease statistics and… swept colon cleansing under the carpet.

So while the top medical doctors are saying that bowel disease is more prevalent than ever, and killing more Americans than ever before, why don't I see more Bowel Detoxification Programs in all the new Natural Healing books being published?

It appears that Natural Healers and these modern day hip medical doctor authors have politely swept it under the carpet and consider it dirty or not high tech. It's like they forget we even have a bowel. They would rather discuss the latest enzyme fad to lose weight or debate how melatonin helps jet lag. The most popular diets today like The Zone (eat the hamburger, but throw the grain bread out) and Atkins (heavy animal protein blood feast) are almost fiberless regimes that left most of my patients constipated to the gills with severely increased cholesterol levels. There is no shortage of hype on St. John's Wort, Cat's Claw, Kava Kava, Colloidal Silver, the latest weight loss amino acid craze or SAM-e. But what about the foundation of health, having a clean colon? Has it become politically incorrect to discuss the bowel?

While these so-called health authors ignore colon cleansing and won't discuss it, millions of Americans are literally rotting from the inside out.

Surgeons remove sections of the colon containing cancerous tumor cells.

CHAPTER THREE
DR. SCHULZE'S CLINIC: THE EARLY YEARS

Armed with my teachers' herbal formulae, I unleashed myself on the world and set up my first real practice in Hollywood, California. But I am afraid nothing could have prepared me for my patients.

I will never forget my first year in practice. I had already healed myself and I had spent ten years traveling around the country following, studying and interning with the best Natural Healers and Herbal Doctors of the past century. I attended their schools, graduated most of them, received two doctorates (17 different diplomas in all) and went on to teach at most of these same schools. To earn money to eat and pay tuition, I worked in most of their clinics and saw patients on the side in massage studios, book stores and the back rooms of health food stores. By now the year

was 1975, and I thought I knew everything. I was definitely over trained and under-experienced.

In the first few weeks of official practice, God sent me a lovely, but very depressed, woman patient about 50 years old. She was partially depressed because of anxiety about the onset of menopause, but mostly because of her daughter. I had heard from another patient that her daughter had a chronic bowel problem, so I asked her to tell me about it and she told me this story.

Her daughter always had trouble going to the bathroom since she was an infant. But when puberty arrived, her bowel just about stopped working altogether. For 2 years, she hardly went to the bathroom at all. At 15, after suffering very long bouts of constipation and almost constant pain in her lower abdomen she finally developed diverticulitis (an infected, herniated, irritated, inflamed, painful bowel) with colon and rectal bleeding. Since medical doctors know nothing about herbs and their healing ability, not even Aloe Vera, they resorted to going up inside this little girl's rear end a few times (an extremely uncomfortable and painful procedure) and cauterized (burned) the inside of her colon in a last ditch effort to try to stop the bleeding. Finally, after six months of torture, they suggested the removal of her bowel, an ileostomy, and said it would save her years of future suffering.

The doctors convinced the family that this was a fairly simple procedure and that many people live a normal comfortable life after having an ileostomy. When the daughter woke up after the surgery in the hospital bed with no bowel, a big red sutured scar from one side of her belly to the other and a hole the size of a silver dollar in her gut with a plastic bag glued on it filled with poop, she was quite freaked out, as you can imagine. The doctors said she would get used to it in no time, but she didn't. After months of depression and not wanting to go to school, her mom decided to throw her a sweet sixteen party to lift her spirits.

Mom invited all of her friends, including a new boyfriend she met at the mall. Mom even sprung for a new party dress. The night of the party came and everything was going great. Towards the end of the party, her daughter was slow dancing with her new boyfriend. They kissed; it was perfect. Then all of a sudden, he shrieked and pushed her away in terror. He was covered with hot, wet, stinking fecal sludge and so was she. Her bag had become unglued and fell off spurting its contents everywhere, covering her, her new party dress and her new boyfriend.

Needless to say, the party was over and the daughter ran to her room in an hysterical, sobbing, crying fit. Mom cleaned her up and tried to console her, but finally decided to let her sleep it off, thinking that tomorrow would be a new day. When mom went up to her daughter's room in the morning, her daughter had hung herself in her closet. She was dead. So much for what the doctors call a simple surgery. What they meant was that it was simple to perform, not simple for the patient to live with. **Some people think that I am acting too much like a hardass when I call the AMA the American**

Murderers Association. Well, if they would have spent a few weeks in my clinic, seeing all the children tortured and killed by modern medicine, they'd call them a lot worse.

As God works, the very next day I got a call from another frantic mom, except this time it wasn't too late. It was Tuesday and the mom told me that her little 11 year-old boy was scheduled for a colostomy surgery (colon removal) on Friday. He had been constipated for years and had not gone in months. She begged me to help, but I only had 2 days in which to work a miracle. I put together a very strong experimental herbal bowel cleanser, because none of the ones my teachers taught me had ever worked for any of my seriously constipated patients. So I got out my old veterinary herbals from the 1800s, and looked up what they would use for large animals like horses. I picked out a few herbs, mixed them up and I gave it to this boy and the very next day he had a bowel movement. Mom called me and told me it was over 2 feet long and up to 2 to 3 inches wide. It was so hard that after numerous failed attempts at flushing it down the toilet, her husband had to go out to the garage and get a shovel and

chop it up to get it to flush. This kid is now a grown man, married, with two kids of his own.

How much do you think his life would have been changed, if not ruined, had he undergone that horrifying, disfiguring surgery? What I used on this little boy was the first crude version of my **Intestinal Formula #1**. Until I refined it, some patients referred to it as TNT Herbal Explosive and Depth Charges. I am strongly against animal torture and experimentation, but I needed to refine my formula. This is when I discovered that relatives are often a great inexpensive replacement for laboratory rats. I gave one of the earliest versions of this formula to my brother, who had a long history of constipation... well, not anymore. I made a mistake with my calculations and gave him a serious overdose. He not only experienced the laws of jet propulsion, but claims that he has never been constipated again and has had perfect bowel movements for the past 25 years. I eventually got the formula perfected. See, up until this point most herbal-bowel formulae available were actually antique herbal medicines. One popular formula used in the 1970s and still sold today in health food stores is Arnold Ehret's Innerclean. This man was born during the civil war and cleansed the bowels of who knows, Buffalo Bill, Wyatt Earp? This formula was designed over 100 years ago when people were riding horses and all food was whole food. One of the other most popular formulas of the 1970s came from one of my great teachers, Dr. John R. Christopher. Naturalax #2 (sometimes referred to as Fennel-B) is a great MILD herbal formula, but he designed this formula during his years of clinical practice, and he died in 1983. So this mild laxative formula is what, 30? 40? 50 years old? My patients in the 1990s were not getting results from this formula either.

From this day on, I vowed to never let another child, or ANYONE, suffer from constipation or have a mutilating colon surgery. This was just one of the reasons I developed my Intestinal Formula #1.

Everyone Poops
By Taro Gomi

Translated by Amanda Mayer Stinchecum

CHAPTER FOUR
CONSTIPATION: THE SHOCKING TRUTH

How much fecal matter can one person hold?

Back in the 1960s, there weren't fiberless fast food restaurants on every street corner and life and work wasn't so sedate. Back then a hard drive was a bumpy ride in a car and not something most of us are typing data into as we sit on our ass all day long. My patients in the 1990s had reached a level of constipation that far exceeded anything Dr. Christopher ever saw in his clinic and way beyond Arnold Ehret's wildest imagination. The average American stores from six to ten pounds of fecal waste in their colon, which is not healthy. As far as the record-breaking accumulation of fecal matter, I had one man in Hawaii who got his dosage up to 46 capsules of my **Intestinal Formula #1**, which is a record in itself, before his bowels moved. Then that night, sitting on the toilet, HE EVACUATED 56 POUNDS OF FECAL MATTER. I met his wife and she said to me that she always knew her husband was full of shit (her words, not mine), but was she right. I had one lady, after doing my **5-Day BOWEL Detox** for a year, lose over 200 pounds. She went from 410 pounds down to 180.

HOW BAD CAN IT GET? CONSTIPATION RECORD BREAKERS

Thirty years ago when I first heard the great Dr. Christopher speak about extreme constipation, I thought he was lying. I wanted to believe him, but when he told me that he had patients that hadn't had a bowel movement in a month, well, I thought that he was telling me a Natural Healing fish story. But, in the first year of running my Hollywood clinic, I had a fashion model come to see me, a very beautiful girl, slim, 5'8" and 115 pounds, and she only had **1 bowel movement a month** for the past year and a half. I was shocked! Where did it go? I was ready to call David Copperfield or Siegfried and Roy. This was real magic.

That year, I had many patients that only had 1 bowel movement a month and for a few years in the clinic that was the record, until a woman came to see me, a 38 year old attorney, that only went every other month. **She had only 6 bowel movements in a year!** She held the record for a while, but then there was a young women from Santa Rosa, California. She only had 3 bowel movements during her last pregnancy. That's one bowel movement per trimester and only two others that year. Now the record holder was **only 5 bowel movements in a year.** That held the record for some time, but three years ago I got a letter from a lady in Southern California thanking me for my **Intestinal Formula #1**. In the letter, she stated that before using my herbal formula she was only having one bowel movement every 6 months. **That is only 2 bowel movements a year, the current record holder!**

Sure, the above were extreme cases, but most of my patients suffered from some sort of constipation. I had well over a thousand patients that were

lucky if they went once a week. People who are constipated live in discomfort, fear and shame. They usually don't go around talking about it and don't know where to turn. Everything has failed them: the empty promises of their medical doctors, their toxic mineral oil, the wimpy herbal laxatives that couldn't even make you fart and the Natural Healers with their bran. Give me a break! They pay the money, and could fill a bus with the bottles of drugs and herbs that they took, **but they still couldn't poop until they met me**.

WHAT THE HECK IS A NORMAL POOP, ANYWAY?

NORMAL FREQUENCY

I have literally traveled around the world in search of what a normal bowel movement and bowel habit should be like. Now, how many people can say that? I have traveled from the remote jungles of Central America to India, China, almost everywhere to discover what is normal, because I knew I wasn't going to find normal in New York, California nor even in Iowa. I wanted to see primitive people living in rural, non-industrialized areas, living simple rural lives under very little stress, getting moderate amounts of exercise and eating simple natural diets of locally foraged food. These relaxed primitive people all seemed to have one bowel movement within 20 to 30 minutes after each major meal that they ate. They just squat, it rapidly comes out within a minute and they are done. No library of magazines, no squeezing, straining, grunting, meditation or prayer. It just came out effortlessly. They seem to average between 2 and 4 bowel movements a day or 14 to 28 bowel movements a week, compared to the average American's bowel habit of 1 bowel movement every 3 to 5 days or 2 to 3 bowel movements a week. **I figured this puts the Average American about 70,000 bowel movements short in their lifetime!**

NORMAL CONSISTENCY

The consistency of your bowel movements should be soft and unformed, like peanut butter or soft serve frozen ice cream. Occasionally, they can be a bit chunky depending on what you ate and how well you chewed it, but in any case they should NOT be formed and they should be light in color. I remember as a kid my dad only went once a week on Sundays. He would take the entire Sunday paper in the bathroom and be in there for hours. When he came out, the room smelled like someone died. I would then take my place at the throne after him and squeeze hard for my once a week bowel movement. Eventually, I would blast out some small black balls as hard as granite. My dad would come into the bathroom to wipe me, but my fecal matter was so dry and hard there was nothing on the toilet paper. I remember my dad remarking, "Now that's a good poop, no wiping, like it's wrapped in cellophane," and I would leave for a week, thinking I did a good job.

SIGNS OF CONSTIPATION

If you need a library in your bathroom, you know, like a stack of magazines on the hamper, then you are constipated. If you drink coffee, well, if you stop, you will also probably stop having bowel movements, too.

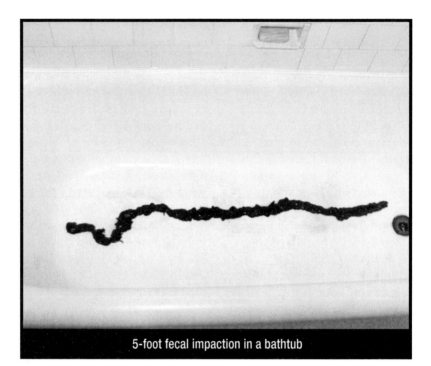

5-foot fecal impaction in a bathtub

A 5-FOOT LONG FECAL IMPACTION

Removed with Dr. Schulze's 5-Day BOWEL Detox

This impaction had been in the patient for many years. Fiberless food sludge that is mostly animal food and refined flour enters your colon. Because of constipation and infrequent bowel movements, it is not completely eliminated. The remainder of it plasters onto the inside wall of your colon. That is why in this picture the fecal casing took on the shape of the inside of this patient's bowel, including the colon's folds and herniated diverticula.

This process can literally go on for decades just like an old steel water pipe that gathers corrosion over years and its inside diameter shrinks. Constipation is a progressively degenerating disease where eventually you have total blockage of the colon or colon disease, often causing cancer and death. I have seen this type of fecal mucoid casing come out of many of the chronically constipated patients in my clinic, but usually not after their first Bowel Detoxification Program. Often, like with this man, it took 4 or 5 times. This man is fine and healthy now, and his lower abdomen that was distended for years is now flat.

I estimate that this was 10 to 15 years of backed up fecal sludge.

PARASITES

Looking under a microscope, anyone can see parasites in animal food. One cubic inch of Grade A Beef often has over 1,000 parasite larva in it. Fish is the worst. Some of their parasites are as big as earth worms. There are even many parasites that live on fruits and vegetables, but if a person has 2 or 3 bowel movements a day, these parasite larva don't hatch, and you're fine. And if you're like me and eat lots of garlic, well, no self-respecting parasite is going to take up house in your colon anyway.

But if you don't have regular bowel movements and only go a few times a week, these parasite larvae hatch, hook onto your colon and start feeding on your backed up waste, and even feed on your tissue. In my clinic, I had every patient do my **5-Day BOWEL Detox**, which is a real parasite flush. After doing it, they would bring in bottles, jugs and pails full of worms, some of them quarts of little worms, many the size of snakes. One of my patients actually went to the hospital after doing my bowel detoxification program because of colon pain. Later, the hospital called me to report that she had evacuated a 35 foot tape worm. WOW!

I could tell a thousand clinical colon parasite war stories, from spaghetti and fettuccini heaps to cobras and rattlesnakes to the things that looked like scorpions and crabs. Maybe I'll just do a parasite issue one day, but for now let's move on.

When you die, the worms actually crawl OUT, not in.

CHAPTER FIVE
HEALING COLON DISEASE NATURALLY

Bowel Cleansing can be the cure for any digestive disease.

Like any great egomaniac student in herbal college, I wanted to develop very intricate and detailed herbal formulae. These formulae would be very difficult to make and could only be made from very exotic and rare herbs found only in the Rainforest or in the Himalayas. And of course, these formulae would be extremely effective for treating very specific diseases. I was going to find the herbal cure for cancer...

Thank God my great teachers deeply ingrained in me that before I could embark on any of my disease specific smart bomb herbal fantasies, I must get my patients on a good health program. First things first. First, I needed to get them following the basics for a month or two, what I now refer to as my Foundational Programs, the foundations of health: a good clean and wholesome food program, thorough bowel cleansing and detoxification, immune boosting, exercise and positive emotional work. I knew that there was no replacement for these basics.

By doing so, I unknowingly destroyed my fancy, disease-specific, herbal formulae dream, because approximately 80% of my patients, regardless of what was wrong with them, regardless of how long they had been sick, got more than relief. THEY GOT WELL! Just from bowel cleansing!

When I added all my other foundational programs, over 95% got well with no specific treatment at all. So much for my trips to Tibet.

You heard right. The vast majority of my patients got

well and recovered from their diseases without ANY specific treatment. All they did was make some common sense lifestyle changes, including cleansing the bowel, and they were healed. My patients, having the nerve to get well before I was ready, ended all my dreams of discovering herbal cures for the afflictions of mankind and turned me into the common sense herbal country doctor that I am today.

BOWEL CLEANSING CAN BE THE CURE FOR ANY DIGESTIVE DISEASE

Bowel cleansing can be very effective for any disease, but especially diseases of the digestive tract. I had many patients heal their upper gastro-intestinal problems like ulcers, hyperacidity, gastric reflux, hiatal hernia and indigestion, plus colon problems such as chronic constipation, spastic colons, colitis and Crohn's disease – and yes, even hemorrhoids. Even liver and gallbladder problems are often relieved, because the same herbs that cleanse and detoxify the bowel also stimulate, cleanse and detoxify the liver and gallbladder.

Many people write me to ask about polyps and bowel cancer, which often go hand in hand. Although I am banned from telling you about my many specific patients healing their serious bowel diseases, like cancers, here is a story I got from an American Botanical Pharmacy customer in San Diego, California a few years ago. He was in his 60s and because of a family history of degenerative bowel disease and colon cancer, his son asked him to go to the doctor and get a sigmoidoscope check – a look into the bowel. This is getting to be a routine check now for older folks, to look for bowel cancer or other bowel disease.

Well, sure enough, they saw it, a big cancer they said looked like a big mushroom growing in his sigmoid colon. It had metastasized and invaded into the muscle, maybe even farther. He also had around 35 polyps. The doctors wanted to admit him to the hospital immediately for a colon resection. They wanted to gut him and carve out at least 12 inches of his colon, probably more. He was very scared.

His son suggested that his dad do my Bowel Cleansing Program. The dad asked the doctor if he could delay the colon surgery for a few months, while he did an herbal bowel cleanse. The doctor said he was nuts, the herbs could be dangerous and even if they weren't they were useless and that a delay of a few days, let alone months, could be suicidal. The cancer would just grow worse, spread, metastasize and kill him.

The dad told me that he was more afraid of the doctors and their surgery. So, he decided to go on my **5-Day BOWEL Detox.** After 8 weeks of bowel cleansing using 8 entire jars of **Intestinal Formula #2**, 3 bottles of **Intestinal Formula #1**, double doses of **SuperFood Plus**, and lots of **Echinacea Plus**, he went back for another look by the doctor. The doctor was furious, and said that surgery may not even save him now, because he delayed getting proper professional treatment by playing around with some hocus-pocus herbs. But when the doctor looked in the colonoscope, he literally shrieked, "Oh my God, I don't believe it!"

Not only were all 35 polyps gone, disappeared, not a trace of even one, but the cancer looked like a dried up skeleton of a cancer. (This is exactly what cancer looks like after your body and especially your white blood cells eat up a tumor.) He

said the doctor then touched the cancer skeleton with a tool through the scope and that it just fell off the walls of the bowel. The CANCER JUST FELL RIGHT OFF!

I had hundreds of patients with bowel polyps that got rid of them. I had many other patients with bowel cancers that disappeared. I had other patients with supposedly unrelated problems like clinical depression, dementia, arthritis, neurological diseases—the list is endless— who all got relief from doing a thorough bowel cleanse.

To actually GET WELL, you have to correct the cause of the disease, and more often than not, it's your bowel.

I had a patient come to me with chronic migraines. They were so severe, that she would even go blind during some of the attacks. Her daughter told me that sometimes she would fall to her knees in public, scream she couldn't take it anymore or even black out and faint. She went to her medical doctor, who gave her some painkillers, and the migraines went away, but eventually they came back. She asked the doctor for something stronger, and he eventually prescribed narcotics. The pain went totally away, but eventually it came back.

She then went to see an Oriental medical doctor who did acupuncture on her, stuck hundreds of needles in her. She said she felt like a human pin cushion. The pain disappeared, but returned.

Out of frustration, she went to a friend's chiropractic doctor who noticed that her cervical vertebrae were subluxated. After a series of adjustments her pain went away, but eventually it came back. Out of desperation she went to a Rolfer, a great system of deep tissue body work, and he did some real restructuring of her neck muscles and tissue, in fact her whole body. The pain was totally gone, but eventually it came back.

Finally, she ended up at an herbalist. He prescribed a classic old herbal formula for pain, actually a great effective formula and one that I used often in my clinic. It was a miracle. Her pain completely disappeared, GONE!

...But eventually it came back.

After 3 years of blinding pain, seeing 16 different doctors and spending thousands of dollars

on everything from electrode stimulators and biofeedback devices to drugs, herbs, vitamins, enzymes, colloidal silver and Noni fruit drink, she finally crawled up to the doorstep of my clinic and told me her story.

Within the first 2 minutes of her very first visit, I asked her one of my favorite questions. How often do you have a bowel movement? It turned out she only went once or twice a week. I suggested that before we do anything, we do a thorough bowel cleansing routine for a couple of weeks. She was furious. She screamed at me and demanded I give her my migraine formula. She was literally sobbing, in tears, begging, pleading for relief. I gave her my **5-Day BOWEL Detox** and sent her home.

After a few days, she called me and told me that her migraines were gone, right after an amazing pooping experience on the toilet, but she was afraid they would return like they had done with ALL the other doctors and practitioners. Over the next few months, I put her through all of my programs and cleaned her colon out a few more times and the migraines have never returned. That was thirteen years ago. The problem with all of the doctors that she saw before me was that they were all focused on the pain in her head, about 3 feet above the real problem.

I had another lady come to see me. She had been out of work, literally flat on her back in pain for 2 1/2 years. She had pain in the lumbar vertebrae, sacrum and sciatic nerve, EVERY DAY, ALL DAY. No work, not even housework, not even going shopping for a few groceries. She was 100% crippled—a total wreck. The medical doctors wanted to fuse her spine, maybe even cut the sciatic nerves to relieve the pain. This is a total dead end. She had many visits to her chiropractor along with Hatha Yoga, which are two of the best therapies for any spinal problem, and especially lower back problems, but she got little results. The osteopaths and orthopedic treatments didn't help either, and she was at her wits end. She even told me she was contemplating killing herself.

Guess what? She was constipated! I put her on the **5-Day BOWEL Detox** and in less than a week all of her pain was gone, and never returned. She was shocked, in disbelief, and she was really, really mad at all the doctors for overlooking something

so simple: constipation. Her blocked, engorged, swollen colon had been pressing on all the nerves in her lower back the whole time.

So even if a person thinks that their particular problem is unrelated to the colon, they might be wrong. A swollen, constipated, irritated bowel puts pressure on and infects everything around it. The nerves from the spine run right next to the bowel before they go down the legs. I have had hundreds of patients with chronic back pain, sciatica and leg pain, and it all disappeared after a good bowel cleansing program.

No matter how far removed the problem seems from the colon, no matter how ridiculous it may seem to do a bowel cleansing program instead of brain surgery, cleanse the bowel first and see what happens.

HOW COULD SO MANY SEEMINGLY UNRELATED HEALTH PROBLEMS BE CAUSED BY CONSTIPATION?

I remember when my older brother got his first car. It was a 1950 Ford station wagon. Of course, it didn't run. What kid's first car did? So it sat in our driveway, and we would sit in it dreaming of the day when we would be burning rubber down the highway. Being more mechanically inclined, I did most of the work on it to get it running.

I used to be able to open up the hood, sit on a front fender with my feet and legs actually dangling inside the engine compartment and work on the engine, change spark plugs, whatever. Get the picture? Big car, big hood, little engine, lots of room. Nowadays, I open up the hood of my current Ford and I just shut it right back up. Every square inch under the hood is jammed, packed with engine parts, power pumps, wires, hoses, pipes and filters. It is too complex, and even if I understood it, there is NO ROOM to work on it. NO SPACE!

What's my point? I used to think our anatomy was like my brother's 1950 Ford. You know, a lung up here, a kidney way down there, a bowel in the middle, with lots of room. Then one day in school, I examined my first cadaver and WOW, what an enlightening experience. The human anatomy is not like my brother's 1950 Ford at all; it is like my modern Ford. Every square inch is packed with something and everything is touching something else. This body of ours must have had some incredible engineer. Everything has its place and THERE IS NO EXTRA ROOM! If one organ swells or gets bigger, then another organ (usually the one next to the swollen one) gets squeezed, compressed or crushed. Organs don't work so well when they are crushed and the blood, lymphatic, nerve and general circulation gets interrupted. Every organ needs good circulation to get nutrition in and get waste out in order to be healthy. Squeezed and compressed organs get sick.

Now the entire colon is so big that it is connected to, touches, sits next to or is in the vicinity of every major organ in the human body except the brain. It also touches most of your major blood vessels and nerves. Constipation causes the colon to literally swell, expand and even herniate. Remember that the leading medical books told us that all of us store too much fecal matter and have this happening inside of us. So when an area of the colon gets constipated and swells, it compresses and crushes the organ next to it. This could be the lungs, the heart, the liver and gallbladder, the pancreas, the kidneys and adrenals, the uterus, the prostate—again, almost every major organ in the body.

This is simply why a constipated, swollen colon can cause an almost endless amount of seemingly unrelated diseases and problems, and I haven't even discussed toxic build-up in the colon that literally infects and poisons nearby organs.

The majority of patients in my clinic were female. Many women could never understand the relationship between their painful periods, PMS, menstrual irregularity, vaginal infections, infertility, menopausal problems, problems during pregnancy, whatever, and their constipation, until I explained that their sigmoid colon wraps around the uterus and that their ovaries are literally attached to the colon. The cure for almost every female problem in my clinic, besides my Female Formulae, was a good bowel cleansing.

Men, don't try to wriggle out of this one. It's the same for you and your prostate, which is attached to your intestines, and the part of your colon that swells and gets constipated most often, crushing and infecting the prostate.

The point is there is NO EXTRA SPACE in your body. If your bowel swells due to constipation and bowel pockets, another organ gets pinched, if not crushed.

What's the bottom line? A sluggish, constipated, swollen bowel, retaining pounds of old fecal matter, can either compress a nearby area and causing disease, or emit infection and toxins which can affect and infect any area of the body.

This explains why many of my patients healed their heart problems, blood pressure problems, breathing problems, blood sugar problems, hormone imbalance problems, fertility problems, liver problems, cholesterol problems, immune problems, urinary problems, adrenal and lack of energy problems, prostate problems, digestive problems, lower back problems, leg circulation and nerve problems by cleaning out their colons, before I ever did any specialized treatment for their problem. This explains why so many of my patients healed their almost infinite list of various diseases by doing my **5-Day BOWEL Detox. My patients healed their brain diseases with colon cleansing proving that you can't have sweet thoughts on a sour stomach.**

I had many patients with Alzheimer's disease and many different types of dementia that turned around and healed themselves after a complete bowel cleanse. And I don't mean people who were just a little foggy and forgetful. I had patients who howled like wolves on the full moon. They were totally insane, but with the aid of their friends, relatives and my herbal programs, they were able to heal themselves and live normal lives.

CLINICAL DEPRESSION HEALED

I had a patient come to me with clinical depression, one of the worse cases I ever saw. He used to be a brilliant man and now he couldn't even speak or get himself dressed.

His family brought him into my clinic, where he sat on the couch in the waiting room with his head sunken and glued into his hands. This poor man was frozen stiff and a tow truck couldn't get him into my examination room. So, I just sent him home. I asked the family to start him on the basics, but all they did was my **5-Day BOWEL Detox**.

Over the next few months, this man evacuated some ungodly stuff. The family said it stunk up the entire house, and even the next door neighbors complained. But to everyone's surprise, this man started coming back to life and within a few months was back to normal and a month or so later back to work. **JUST BY CLEANING OUT HIS COLON!**

Everyone wants a quick cleanse. Sure, party for a decade and then try to clean up the whole mess in a few minutes. It's not going to happen.

Any cleansing or detoxification program is a TOTAL JOKE, unless you do a thorough bowel cleansing for a few weeks FIRST!

NEVER, NEVER, NEVER UNDERESTIMATE THE POWER OF COLON CLEANSING

When I ran my clinic, new patients were often upset when I told them we had to start with a thorough colon cleansing. What they wanted was my secret energy pill, youth pill or something to make their insomnia, infertility, back spasms, headaches, diabetes, arthritis, whatever, miraculously go away.

Natural Healing is NOT about temporary quick fixes or pills to mask symptoms. It is NOT about cutting, poisoning and burning out disease. That's what medical doctors do. When you take that approach, often out of nowhere, your disease returns with a vengeance, much worse the second time around.

Natural Healing is about getting to the root cause of disease and illness, correcting it, and then building a healthy lifestyle so your body can do its best healing possible. Then, you can enjoy a long, healthy and energetic life.

NATURAL HEALING IS NOT ABOUT DR. SCHULZE HEALING PEOPLE. IT'S ABOUT... PEOPLE HEALING THEMSELVES

So, I had to kick some butt and do some convincing to get my patients to understand why a belly full of old poisonous, toxic fecal waste and sluggish elimination was probably the cause of their problem. If it wasn't the direct cause, it was surely an indirect one.

You should have seen the surprised looks on all of their faces when after completing my **5-Day BOWEL Detox**, their aches and pains were gone. About 80% had total relief from their health problems without addressing them directly.

MY PATIENTS THOUGHT I WAS FATHER SCHULZE NOT DR. SCHULZE

Most of my patients came into my clinic with a very guilty conscience regarding their lifestyle. They wanted to repent their sins of junk food and debauched living. They thought I could just wave my hands over them and have them say a few "Hail Tofus" and everything would be OK. Well, it's not quite that simple. Most had already tried some kind of detox on their own, with either **no results or bad results**. Everyone nowadays is selling some **quick detox**. There are a few problems here.

First, don't fool yourself. It takes most of us 20 or 30 years of rough and tough living, before we develop a disease. So, you're not going to heal yourself in 24 hours.

Secondly, I made my patients EARN the right to do a detox program. The reason for this is simple. When you start any detoxification program, what happens is that you dislodge and dissolve poisons and toxins that have built up in your fat and muscle cells and in various organs. During an effective detox, when these wastes are dissolved they are deposited into your colon for rapid elimination from your body. If you are constipated or not having regular frequent bowel movements, these poisons sit there, can reabsorb and make you really sick. This is why many people who undertake a detox program without first making sure their colon is working, feel weak, shaky, nauseous, headachy or HORRIBLE. I had patients that literally almost died doing intensive detoxification programs with hot saunas, gallons of juices, herbs, whatever, but hadn't had a bowel movement in weeks and the detoxification almost killed them.

This is why BEFORE you even think about any intensive detoxification program, THE COLON MUST BE ACTIVELY WORKING AND CLEAN!

FIRST THINGS FIRST!

This is worth repeating. The first step in any health program, especially BEFORE any blood and lymphatic cleansing or detoxification program, is to cleanse and detoxify the bowel. You must make sure it is working frequently and effectively and also make sure all of the old, toxic fecal material is out of the colon. Then you will enjoy an effective detoxification program, feel great while you're doing it and get the most out of it.

So the first step is my 5-Day BOWEL Detox discussed in the next chapter...

"The first and most
Important Step
for preventing
and healing disease
is Bowel Cleansing."
— *Dr. Richard Schulze*

Dr. Schulze's
5-Day BOWEL Detox

- ▸ **Have more ENERGY, feel lighter and have a flatter stomach**

- ▸ **A powerful intestinal vacuum that draws out old toxic fecal matter**

- ▸ **Eliminate constipation and promote regular, healthy and complete bowel movements**

CHAPTER SIX
Dr. Schulze's
5-Day BOWEL Detox

Remember...Cleansing your colon is THE most important first step to better health.

Today, more than 100,000 people worldwide have used this very simple and effective program to eliminate constipation, cleanse their colon, detoxify their body and heal and prevent colon disease.

No matter how far removed your current health problem seems from your colon, cleanse the bowel FIRST and see what happens. **If you're like my patients, you will be thrilled with the results.**

A POWERFUL, EFFECTIVE AND COMPLETE CLEANSING PROGRAM FOR THE COLON

The first step to powerful health and the best way to prevent disease is to clean out and detoxify your colon on a regular basis. Of further importance is to train your bowel

to empty itself on a regular basis, 30-60 minutes after every main meal, two to three times a day. My **5-Day BOWEL Detox** will help you achieve both of these goals.

HOW TO BEGIN:

The first thing you must determine before you begin this program is how often you have a bowel movement. That will decide how you start.

START HERE – If you are currently skipping days without having a bowel movement...

90 Ct.   250 Ct.

...start using the **Intestinal Formula #1** only. It is best not to rush and not to use the **Intestinal Formula #2** *right away*. Let's get your bowel working better first. The reason for this is simple. You are already a bit constipated and sluggish. Your bowel is not active enough to use the **Intestinal Formula #2**, which could constipate you even further. Don't worry, there are more than enough **Intestinal Formula #1** capsules in your bottle to do this *and* complete the entire **5-Day BOWEL Detox**.

So start by taking one capsule of **Intestinal Formula #1** with or just after dinner. It is best to take this formula with food. If the next morning you do not have a good, complete bowel movement, or none at all, this evening take two capsules with or just after dinner. Continue to increase the dosage of **Intestinal Formula #1** by one capsule each evening until the next morning, when you sit on the toilet, you have a complete bowel movement. A complete bowel movement may consist of a larger volume than you would normally see in the toilet bowl, or you may experience two or three intestinal waves of fecal matter elimination. So don't be too quick to get off the toilet. Your bowel movement may also be loose, even a bit like liquid at first. You may also experience a

bit of gas or cramping. All of this is normal.

When you are having one or more bowel movements a day for an entire week, without skipping, you may now begin taking the **Intestinal Formula #2** (follow the directions on the next page). You must continue using the **Intestinal Formula #1** at your current dosage and even increase your dosage by one or two capsules when you begin the **Intestinal Formula #2**.

START HERE—If you are currently having one or more bowel movements a day...

Capsules

Packets

...then you are ready to start using **Intestinal Formula #2**, along with **Intestinal Formula #1**.

If you are taking **Intestinal Formula #2** capsules, then take ten capsules, five times a day, for the next five days. If you are taking **Intestinal Formula #2** packets, then take one packet, five times a day, for the next five days. During this program, on average, you will be taking the **Intestinal Formula #2** (capsules or powder) every two to three hours.

Follow dosage directions on product. Remember, when taking **Intestinal Formula #2** capsules or powder, you must drink a minimum of 16 ounces of liquid with each dose. You may drink pure water, herbal tea or fresh fruit or vegetable juice.

IMPORTANT!

While taking **Intestinal Formula #2**, continue taking one or more capsules of the **Intestinal Formula #1** every evening, with dinner or just after dinner. Most people under 150 lbs. need only one capsule, while those over 150 lbs. usually need two capsules. Intestinal Formula #1 does many things for your bowel, but most importantly it removes all the accumulated **Intestinal Formula #2** from your bowel the next morning.

NOTE: If on the morning after taking your **Intestinal Formula #2** you do not have a bowel movement, increase your liquid intake today and also increase your dosage of **Intestinal Formula #1** this evening by one additional capsule.

IMPORTANT HELPFUL TIPS

TIP #1: EDUCATE YOURSELF

If you are unfamiliar with what is normal bowel frequency or normal fecal consistency, you may think that something is wrong at first. You may also experience abdominal feelings that you have not experienced before. What you are used to is not normal or healthy.

TIP #2: DON'T BE IN A HURRY

It took you years to become constipated, so take a few weeks or a month using my **Intestinal Formula #1** to get your bowel regulated, before you begin doing my complete **5-Day BOWEL Detox** using **Intestinal Formula #2**.

There is no maximum dosage of **Intestinal Formula #1**. The record so far is 48 capsules in one day, so I am sure you haven't reached that dosage yet. Many people need six, eight or even 12 capsules a day to get their bowel working normally. But, remember to increase by only one capsule daily. This way you won't accidentally discover the "laws of jet propulsion."

TIP #3: SPECIAL ADVICE FOR PEOPLE WITH A "HOT" METABOLISM

If you are prone to having a "hot" bowel, diarrhea, colitis, bowel inflammation, Crohn's disease, etc., then you are better off with "cool" detoxifiers, such as my **Intestinal Formula #2**. You may never need, or be able to tolerate, my **Intestinal Formula #1**. Stay with **Intestinal Formula #2** and use it periodically for a week or a month at a time.

FINAL NOTE

As a child, I had only one bowel movement a week. That was normal for everyone in my family. Also normal for my family was severe bouts of constipation, hemorrhoids, kidney stones, heart attacks and cancer.

It took me 12 years of using my **Intestinal Formula #1** and consistent bowel cleansing to get my bowel working normally. Then for the last 20 years, I have done my **5-Day BOWEL Detox** about every season, 3 or

4 times a year. I currently have 2 to 3 bowel movements a day, 20 to 30 minutes after every main meal of perfect consistency.

My point is that just because I inherited a dysfunctional, constipated bowel didn't mean I had to live with the suffering and illness that it caused me. With this exact program, I was able to clean out and train my bowel to work perfectly. For me and my patients, great health was something we had to earn.

If you have never before cleaned out your bowel and have now done my 5-Day BOWEL Detox, CONGRATULATIONS! This is a great start to a healthier life. I'll say it again, this program is VERY SIMPLE!

INTESTINAL FORMULA #1

90 Ct.   250 Ct.

▸ **Promotes regular, healthy and complete bowel movements**

▸ **Stimulates and strengthens the muscular movement of your colon**

▸ **The best bowel cleanser on the planet**

Botanical Ingredients:

Curacao & Cape Aloe Leaf, Senna Leaves & Pods, Cascara Sagrada Aged Bark, Barberry Rootbark, Ginger Rhizome, Garlic Bulb, African Bird Pepper

Intestinal Formula #1 stimulates your colon's natural muscle action and strengthens the muscles of the large intestine. It relieves constipation. It also halts putrefaction and disinfects, soothes and heals, improves digestion, relieves gas and cramps, increases the flow of bile which in turn cleans the gall bladder, bile ducts and liver, destroys Candida albicans overgrowth and promotes a healthy intestinal flora. It also destroys parasites, increases circulation and is anti-bacterial, anti-viral and anti-fungal.

The herbs in this formulae, like Aloe, Senna and Cascara Sagrada all contain the natural phytochemical (plant chemical) called Emodin, which increases peristaltic waves, the propulsive contractions of the colon muscle. Oregon Grape Root stimulates and flushes the liver, the gallbladder and the production of bile. Garlic is anti-bacterial, anti-viral and anti-fungal. Habanero and Ginger are both powerful stimulants to the colon. Habanero will also correct intestinal bleeding.

If your bowels are irritated, inflamed, hot or working too frequently, skip **Intestinal Formula #1** and go directly to **Intestinal Formula #2** (see next page).

INTESTINAL FORMULA #2

Capsules

Packets

▸ **A powerful intestinal vacuum that draws out old fecal matter, toxins, poisons, bacteria, drug residues, mercury and lead**

▸ **A strong anti-inflammatory and soothing agent**

Botanical Ingredients:

Flax Seed, Apple Fruit Pectin, Pharmaceutical Grade Bentonite Clay, Psyllium Seed & Husk, Slippery Elm Inner Bark, Marshmallow Root, Fennel Seed, Activated Willow Charcoal

Intestinal Formula #2 is a strong purifier and intestinal vacuum. It draws old, hardened fecal matter off the walls of your colon and out of any diverticula.

Intestinal Formula #2 contains the three most powerful and effective absorbers and neutralizers known: clay, charcoal and pectin.

Our Pharmaceutical Grade Bentonite Clay will actually absorb up to forty times its weight in intestinal fecal matter and waste. It also smothers and draws out intestinal parasites. The Activated Willow Charcoal is the greatest absorbing agent for every toxin and poison known. It will absorb and render harmless over 3,000 known drug residues, pesticides, insecticides and just about every harmful chemical known. This is why it is the active ingredient in nearly every water filter made today. Apple Pectin draws numerous harmful substances out of your intestines, especially heavy metals like mercury and lead, and carcinogenic radioactive materials.

The addition of Marshmallow Root along with Psyllium Seed and Flax Seed makes the formula mucilaginous as well as demulcent. Mucilaginous means that all the water and herbs can sit in your bowel, soaking against the internal wall of your colon, softening and breaking up old, dried and hardened fecal waste that may have been in you for years. Demulcent means it will also ease the pain and suffering of a hot, irritated and inflamed intestinal mucous membrane. It literally heals the tissue! From stomach ulcers to colitis, Crohn's disease, IBS, spastic colons, and all types of inflammatory bowel diseases, mucilaginous and demulcent herbs are the healing answer.

Your body knows how to heal itself from every disease. All it needs is your help

CHAPTER SEVEN
ADDITIONAL PRODUCTS AND PROGRAMS
TO AID DIGESTION AND ELIMINATION

From heartburn and acid reflux to motion sickness and food poisoning, these are the formulae and programs I developed in my clinic to keep your entire digestive tract operating smoothly.

24-HOUR BOWEL DETOX

▸ **Quickly and easily removes dangerous micro-organisms and keeps them out of your body, stomach and bloodstream**

▸ **A powerful one-day detox that captures, neutralizes and eliminates toxins in your bowel**

Program Includes:
*6 Intestinal Formula #1 &
50 Intestinal Formula #2 Capsules*

This is a great tune-up for those that have already done my **5-Day BOWEL Detox**.

Anyone who has done my **5-Day BOWEL Detox** knows the power of doing it for just one day. Maybe you ate food that you don't usually eat or too many desserts or you ate at that not-so-clean restaurant with suspect food and you want all this merchandise out of you right now! You want to capture it, absorb it and get it out before it gets into the rest of your body.

My **24-Hour BOWEL Detox** is for anyone who needs a fast and easy detox to STOP whatever is in their bowel from getting into their body and bloodstream.

Whether you are living it up or just living life, there are a thousand reasons to cleanse and detoxify your bowel. If you can't commit to my **5-Day BOWEL Detox** or only have a day or two, then my **24-Hour BOWEL Detox** is just right for you. Many people, myself included, only do this detox for a day, just to either remove—or repent for—our overeating and food choice sins.

Whether you are having toxic mercury fillings removed at the dentist, have just been in a toxic environment, ate weird food at an even weirder restaurant, the kids are sick with the stomach flu or you had some bad seafood or potato salad. Whether you are traveling to far away lands or your local restaurant, these are all reasons to have my **24-Hour BOWEL Detox** ALWAYS on hand. I always throw one in my suitcase when packing for a trip.

This one-day detox will immediately get anything in your bowel neutralized, captured and detoxified immediately and it will be out of your body the very next morning, guaranteed!

INTESTINAL FORMULA #3

4 ounces

▸ **Promotes soft and easy bowel movements**

▸ **Strengthens colon muscles**

▸ **Tastes great to kids of all ages**

Botanical Ingredients:
Senna Leaf & Pod, Cascara Sagrada Aged Bark, Anise Seed, Clove Bud, Tangerine Oil, California Fig Concentrate

This formula is a great-tasting, liquid laxative for the whole family. Although I originally designed this herbal colon cleanser primarily for children, it's strong enough for adults, too. In fact, many adults prefer it instead of **Intestinal Formula #1,** because it has a milder action.

Every year, hundreds of parents brought their babies, toddlers and children into my clinic. Some were very constipated. I had some babies that were so constipated, they had fecal matter backed up into their stomachs. One little eight-month-old baby in my clinic, who was actually scheduled for colostomy surgery, actually regurgitated fecal matter. I am happy to say that this child never had the surgery.

In the clinic, I saw hundreds of children and teenagers with extreme constipation. This formula saved all of them from torturous, disfiguring and life-altering colon surgeries. In fact, all of these constipated kids improved in just a day or two after starting this formula.

Like my **Intestinal Formula #1**, my **Intestinal Formula #3** also contains Senna Leaf and Pod and Cascara Sagrada Aged Bark. Both contain the natural phytochemical (plant chemical) called Emodin, which increases the normal muscular contractions (peristalsis) of the gastro-intestinal tract, especially the colon. This formula promotes soft, easy bowel movements and it will help strengthen the colon for better future elimination.

Figs and prunes have been used effectively as a natural treatment for constipation since the beginning of recorded medical history. The base of this tonic, California Fig concentrate, acts not only as a mild natural laxative, but also makes the formula sweet and taste good for the kids.

Anise Seed and Clove Bud are strong carminatives and antispasmodics and therefore are used to relieve gas, cramps, colic, indigestion, nausea and stomach aches. Tangerine Oil is anti-bacterial, but is also used to mask and flavor the formula.

You can't have SWEET THOUGHTS on a sour stomach.

DIGESTIVE TONIC

1 ounce

- ▸ **Stops indigestion, gas and stomach upsets immediately**

- ▸ **Eliminates the discomfort that sometimes comes with traveling and motion**

- ▸ **Freshens breath**

- ▸ **Great for kids with sensitive digestion**

Botanical Ingredients:
Ginger Rhizome, Sweet Fennel Seed, Peppermint Leaf & Peppermint Essential Oil

In this formula, I combined three of the most effective and powerful carminative herbs, Jamaican Ginger Rhizome, Sweet Fennel Seed and Peppermint Leaf and Essential Oil. These three herbs make a powerful tonic that relieves gas, cramps, colic, bloating, heartburn, indigestion, nausea and pain in the digestive tract, especially the stomach. This is the greatest formula for anyone who has any digestive problem.

Ginger Rhizome, Sweet Fennel Seed and Peppermint Leaf all contain essential oils that, according to medical texts and even the Merck Index, are therapeutically carminative, which means they stimulate the digestive system, as well as relax the stomach, thereby supporting the digestion and helping relieve gas in the digestive tract. Ginger is a powerful anti-emetic (reduces nausea and relieves or prevents vomiting), while Peppermint is an effective gastric sedative and antispasmodic.

This is a great formula for when you wake up in the middle of the night with acid reflux, indigestion or heartburn. A few droppersful of this formula in a little water and in five minutes your indigestion will be gone, and then it's back to dreamland.

When you are out and you eat that meal that **feels like a rock in your stomach**, this formula will be a Godsend. You can even add a few droppersful to a cup of hot water and make a tasty digestive tea.

Also, when traveling, this is the **greatest formula for motion sickness.** I know, because I have traveled all over the world on all types of transportation. From jumbo jets through storms over the North Atlantic and hovercraft across the turbulent English Channel and North Sea, to rickshaws in India and swaying camels in North Africa, I have been on some very bumpy, swaying, and shaky rides. I always bring along my **Digestive Tonic** and ride it out with a smile.

BOWEL FLUSH "SHOT"

▸ **NEUTRALIZES and STOPS bloating, gas and digestive upsets**

▸ **ENSURES a complete emptying of your bowel and digestive system by the following morning**

Herbal Ingredients:

Dr. Schulze's Proprietary Cathartic Formulae: Senna Leaf & Pod, Cascara Sagrada Aged Bark, **Dr. Schulze's Proprietary Carminative Formulae:** *Hawaiian Yellow Ginger Root, Peppermint Leaf & Oil, Anise Seed,* **Dr. Schulze's Proprietary WormEx Formulae:** *Agrimony Herb, Black Walnut Hulls, Cinchona Bark, Clove Bud, Goldenseal Root Thyme Leaf in a base of Organic Prune & Fig Concentrate, Tangerine Oil*

After three decades in my clinic and tens of thousands of patients, I learned a few things. The first is, we are not perfect. Maybe your day started with a bad breakfast, doughnuts or pancakes or bacon and eggs, all of which you know you shouldn't eat. You grab a junk food lunch on the run or a candy bar and a cup of coffee. For dinner, you were out of control and ate a half of loaf of bread, before your dinner even arrived. Then, you ate the surf and turf and the Crème Brulee. All you ate today was grease, fat, sugar, calories, cholesterol, free radicals, heavy metals, toxic chemicals and toxic food and now, you're exhausted, bloated, guilty, sick to your stomach and literally full of crap.

DR. SCHULZE'S BOWEL FLUSH "SHOT" TO THE RESCUE!

Now, you can eliminate your digestive nightmare and relax and get a good night's sleep. And first thing in the morning, all of this garbage will be out of you. This new herbal "SHOT" is for those times when we overindulge, eat food we know we shouldn't or just eat too much. Whether it was Mom's famous meatballs, Dad's backyard barbeque, Aunt Betty's cookies, a friend's "pot luck" or simply a night out of fast food, junk food, greasy food or mystery food. Look, its bad enough what you ate and how much you ate, but let's not suffer anymore. STOP beating yourself up and let's just get it out of you and START over.

INTESTINAL FORMULA #1 - MAX

▸ **PROMOTES regular, healthy and complete bowel movements**

▸ **STIMULATES and STRENGTHENS the muscular movement of the colon**

▸ **New STRONGER and more POWERFUL formula**

Herbal Ingredients:
Curaçao & Cape Aloe Leaf, Senna Leaf & Pod, Cascara Sagrada Aged Bark, Hawaiian Yellow Ginger Root, Habanero Pepper

This new MAXIMUM STRENGTH version of my Intestinal Formula #1 is for those who are taking more than 4 capsules a day of my original Intestinal Formula #1, and who need something even stronger and more effective. This is a very potent formula for those who chronically suffer from constipation and need relief right away.

ABOUT THE HERBS IN THIS FORMULA:

Cape & Curaçao Aloes, Senna Leaf & Pod & Cascara Sagrada Aged Bark

These herbs have all been used for centuries, if not millennia, to stimulate and tone the muscles of the large intestine to be stronger, and promote more complete and more frequent bowel elimination. Because these herbs offer so many health benefits, they were considered almost magical by the many cultures, who have used them and referred to them as Miracle Healers and Sacred Barks.

Ginger Root

This herb is a powerful carminative, that relieves gas and bloating in your intestinal tract.

Habanero Pepper

These peppers dramatically increase blood circulation flow and are a wonderful remedy for the intestines.

DIGESTIVE "SHOT"

▸ **PROMOTES better digestion**

▸ **PREVENTS digestive disturbances**

▸ **COMBATS gas, bloating and nighttime digestive upsets**

Herbal Ingredients:
Dr. Schulze's Proprietary Digestive Formulae: Hawaiian Yellow Ginger Root, Peppermint Leaf & Oil, Fennel Seed.
Dr. Schulze's Proprietary Digestive Enzyme Formulae: Papaya Purée With Enhanced Papain Enzyme, Pineapple Purée & Bromelain Enzyme

My new Digestive "SHOT" contains 10 droppersful of my Digestive Tonic—and this is the amount I would have given you if you came to my clinic with a digestive disturbance, like gas, bloating, indigestion…anything. You'll notice it when you take it that it's POWERFUL and it WORKS. It's a "WOW!"

This "SHOT" is to be used on an as needed basis, taken before a meal to assist, aid and promote better digestion and after a meal or before bed to prevent any digestive disturbances.

This herbal complex contains the three most powerful "digestive aid" herbs known: Peppermint Spirits, Ginger Rhizome and Sweet Fennel Seeds. PLUS, I added my enhanced Papain Papaya puree, and also enhanced Bromelain Pineapple puree. Both Papain and Bromelain are powerful digestive enzymes. Together, they help break down food, while your body is trying to also break down the food in your digestive tract. They almost pre-digest the food for you.

This is a good tonic to have on your nightstand for those times when you go out and have a lunch or a dinner that didn't agree with you. It would be a great idea to take the entire "SHOT" before you go to bed. If you didn't and you wake up in the middle of night with that horrible burning in your throat, well, take the "SHOT" now. You can take it either before bed or if you wake up in trouble. Shake it up, and take the entire "SHOT", and what you're going to notice is you're going to be able to go right back to sleep.

CHAPTER EIGHT
SIX NATURAL WAYS TO GET YOUR COLON WORKING AGAIN

Here are some ways to stimulate your bowel.

People always forget the simple things that our grandparents knew. Often with patients, I would just get them to soak some prunes. I mean, when my plum trees ripen here in my orchard I don't get one a day, I get four thousand in an hour. And then, the tree is bare three days later. So often what fruit is telling you is gorge on it, have massive amounts for a short period of time, do a plum cleanse. With prunes, you can just soak them in water, put them in a blender, add some apple juice, and for some people that's enough. I found that for my patients most of them needed something to jump-start the engine, something to get that bowel working effectively. But there's basically six natural ways to get your colon working.

The first one is to drink more liquid. The bowel can't work properly without a minimum of two quarts, or sixty-four ounces of liquid, in a day. The fastest way to get your bowel to stop working is to dehydrate yourself. Your bowel needs water in order to process the fecal matter and get it out of your body. The second one is to eat more fiber. Fiber makes your bowel work. Sludge doesn't. Animal foods are sludge. Refined flour products are sludge. We have to eat more fruits, vegetables, grains and sprouts. Adding more fiber and drinking more liquid can make your bowel work tremendously better. And the least altered something is from its natural form (the more raw it is), the more powerful it is. Then there are the natural laxative foods, like fruit. Fruits are great. Apples, dates, figs, bananas, just about any food that contains liquid. Stay away from the dehydrated fruits if you're constipated, because they suck moisture out of your body and we're trying to add more in. The fourth way is to move your body. Just walking creates peristalsis. Sexual intercourse creates peristalsis. Next are the positive emotions. You have to think positively. If you hate yourself, if you're filled with fear, that's a good way to shut your bowel down totally. And the last one is to get into the herbs. Herbs are foods, too. Start using some herbs to get your bowel stimulated.

❶ DRINK MORE LIQUID.

You need to drink at least 2 quarts of liquid a day, if not more. Anything less than 64 ounces (2 quarts) of liquid a day doesn't give your fecal matter enough hydration to come out normally and easily. So in other words, your fecal matter gets too hard and has a hard time leaving your body. Dehydration is the number one cause of constipation. The best liquids for you to drink are pure water (never tap water), herb tea and diluted fruit and vegetable juices.

❷ EAT MORE FIBER.

You have to eat food with more fiber in it. There is no fiber in any animal food or any animal by-products. Let's make it clear—there is ZERO FIBER in any meat, chicken, fish, eggs, dairy, cheese or any other animal food. Fiber makes you poop, it is that simple. Fiber is only found in NON-ANIMAL foods. So you want a high fiber vegetarian food program: fruits, vegetables, nuts, seeds, grains, beans and legumes. That's where the fiber is.

❸ EAT NATURAL LAXATIVE FOODS.

Apples, bananas, figs and dates are famous. Did you forget about PRUNES? Fresh, juicy organic fruits that have a high water content are always better than dried, but even dried fruits can be of help. As with tip #2 above, all non-animal food is fibrous, but grains are naturally very fibrous and help the bowels move. Go on a raw food program for a few days and you won't have to worry about constipation at all, but you might need to make a map of all the nearest bathrooms.

❹ MOVE YOUR BODY.

All movement excites peristaltic muscular waves, the muscular contraction of the bowel. Exercise will get your bowels working again. I'm not talking sit-ups, I'm talking walking, breathing, laughing, running, dancing, yoga, swimming, anything, but you've got to get up and move around.

❺ POSITIVE EMOTIONS.

We have to reduce our stress level. Stress, fear and hate are strong emotions that will cause people to get constipated more than eating ten pounds of cheese a day. We have to learn how to release our stress. Laugh more, learn some jokes. Do some deep breathing during the day. Develop positive emotional habits and learn positive emotional phrases like "I love myself" and "I love my life." You must learn that EVERYTHING is a blessing from God and even if it seems bad now, it is just because you can't see the whole picture. **Tomorrow is what you Believe and Do Today.**

❻ MY 5-DAY BOWEL DETOX.

Never underestimate the power of colon cleansing. My **5-Day BOWEL Detox** is EASY, SIMPLE to do and extremely EFFECTIVE. In the clinic, I witnessed thousands of patients have a dramatic change in their lives, just by doing this bowel program. Approximately 80% of my patients healed themselves by just doing this program. Again...

Never, NEVER underestimate the HEALING POWER of colon cleansing.

CHAPTER NINE
ALL ABOUT DIARRHEA

What it is, how it happens, and the natural cures...

We have all heard the old kids' baseball song, "*When your sliding into home and you fill your pants with foam,* DIARRHEA!" Well, Diarrhea isn't really a laughing matter. Most people don't know it's genetic. That's right, it runs in your jeans. OK, enough with the diarrhea jokes.

Seriously, most people have experienced it and know what it feels like, but they really don't know what it actually is let alone what causes it, why your body is doing it and most important, how to treat it, *naturally*. Well, read this chapter and you will be prepared the next time you or a loved one gets it.

WHAT CAUSES DIARRHEA?

What we call diarrhea is actually the end result of poisoning.

Diarrhea in America is most often caused by food poisoning. Although there are stomach and intestinal virus, in my clinic, what my patients often referred to as the 24-hour stomach flu, was actually just plain and simple food poisoning. The most common types are bacterial poisoning from fish, especially sushi (raw fish) and from chicken, although any type of dead animal flesh or milk is a bacterial breeding ground nightmare and can cause it.

When traveling to third world countries, diarrhea may feel the same, but the cause is a bit different. In fact, it is so common in many countries they have many colorful slang names for it like "Montezuma's Revenge" or the "Mexican Hat Dance" in Mexico or Central America, and "Delhi Belly" in India or the "Katmandu Quickstep" in Nepal. Regardless of its name, and how you ingested it, it is almost always caused by accidentally ingesting other people's fecal matter.

The most common way to get it is simply by drinking contaminated water or even the ice in your drinks or droplets of water on a washed glass. It can also be on any type of food. I know this is gross, but one of the triumphs of the civilized world and modern public health is that we have succeeded in separating our feces from our water supply, and the general environment for that matter. The country you are visiting and surroundings may look very different, but the micro-organisms that cause traveler's diarrhea are pretty much the same organisms worldwide. The reason that we get diarrhea when we travel is simply that peoples' stool is more available in the environment: drinking water, on the street, on people's hands, on flies and on the food itself. So the main way to get traveler's diarrhea is by consuming organisms that have grown in someone else's intestines. In other words, you have to eat someone else's stool. In almost all developing nations, fecal matter is so widely strewn in the environment, it is almost impossible to avoid.

Recently, diarrhea caused by parasites is becoming so prevalent, it may surpass bacterial diarrhea. And, diarrhea caused by viral infections that lurk on cruise ships has also been rising dramatically.

The absolute best safeguard against getting diarrhea, whether due to bacteria, parasites or virus, is to always drink bottled water, which is available *everywhere* today. Contaminated water is the number one way people get infected. If no bottled water is available, which is extremely rare, you can use all types of water filters sold in backpacking, camping and survival stores. A last ditch effort is to boil and strain your water before drinking. Also wash your hands every hour and wash everything you eat, and don't eat out, especially at street vendors or street cafes. But no matter how careful you are, in many countries you are almost certain to get it regardless of how careful you are, but you won't get it as frequently or as bad, if you follow my advice. In countries like India and the many countries in Africa and Asia, you will probably get it within the first few days. Don't worry, later I will tell you how to heal it and be comfortable almost immediately.

WHAT IS GOING ON IN YOUR BODY?

I know that most Americans think of diarrhea as a disease, so it's a surprise to them when I tell them that it is actually another beautiful and miraculous way that your body is protecting your health and taking care of you. Let's face it, in America most of what we know about health has been advertising from the beef, dairy and junk food industries, and most of what we know about disease has been the onslaught of magazine and television ads from the pharmaceutical industry. In other words, most of what we know about health and disease, we are told by someone who is trying to sell us something. So the information may be a bit slanted, if not totally absurd. For this reason I will not mention any of my products in this article until the end in a special section titled, "Natural Cures For Diarrhea", OK.

"Diarrhea is a natural protective function of your body. It is a response to intestinal poisoning. Normally, most of the water is removed from your fecal matter by your colon, which creates a normal partially formed stool. But when your immune sensors in your intestinal tract (the Peyer's patches and appendix) detect harmful toxic bacteria or micro-organisms, they immediately force your bowels to evacuate all its contents *before* the water is removed, while your feces is still in liquid form. This is done to remove toxic bacteria from your body, IMMEDIATELY, *before* it could penetrate your organs and hurt you, or EVEN KILL YOU."

When we consume any liquid or food that is toxic to our body, bacteria, virus, fungus, parasites, any poison, we have numerous ways that our body detects it and neutralizes, kills and eliminates it *long before* the poison reaches our bowel. The tonsils are an immune aggregation and can detect all types of harmful organisms that enter our mouths and create an immune response against them. And if the tonsils miss them, well, just the PH of our digestive juices, the liver's bile or the pancreas' hydrochloric acid is enough to destroy just about any bug. We have numerous other passive and active defense mechanisms in our digestive tract long before any toxic micro-organism can reach our bowel, but if there are enough of them and they are resilient and toxic enough, well, sometimes they can reach there.

If they make it, they are often detected in the small intestine by the immune aggregation, a mass of immune system tissue called the Peyer's patches. Upon entering the illeocecal valve, the entrance to your colon, the first stop in your large intestine is the cecum. Perfectly placed in the very bottom of your cecum, the first resting place for feces in your colon is the **appendix**.

Your appendix is the immune aggregation of your colon. Again, an immune aggregation is the same as your tonsils, a mass of immune tissue and white blood cells ready and waiting to defend you against any attacker. Well, when the appendix detects any harmful organism that is still alive, that made it past all of your many immune defenses, well then it knows that this is either a lot of poison or very strong and harmful micro-organisms. So what do *you* think the best thing for the appendix to tell *your* bowel would be? Hold on to all of this disease causing and potentially lethal poison, or get rid of it as soon as possible. That's right, to get this poison out of you the fastest way possible, to empty your bowels contents *before* you assimilate the water out of your feces, while your feces are still in a liquid state. So your body forces you to evacuate your very wet and watery feces as fast as possible, to protect you from assimilating any more poison. This is diarrhea.

Diarrhea is a general term to describe when a person's stools are more liquid or more frequent than normal. In America, having 2 to 3 regular bowel movements a day, that are soft and not black *hard as granite balls*, is considered by some to be diarrhea, even though this is what normal bowel movements should be like. Diarrhea is when you have many fluid stools in a short period of time. The word comes from the Greek meaning "*to flow through*". Dysentery, another word originating from the Greek, meaning "*bad intestine*" (the Greeks must have had a lot of diarrhea and dysentery) is when there is evidence that the harmful micro-organisms have invaded and perforated your intestinal wall and you will most often see pus, mucus and blood in the liquid stool, and be in a lot of pain and cramping. Although the words diarrhea and dysentery are often commonly interchanged, medically there is a strong dividing line between the two. Diarrhea can easily turn into dysentery, especially by going against what your body is naturally trying to do and by using medical treatment and using drugs.

Diarrhea is uncomfortable, painful, inconvenient, cramping, watery, foul-smelling, liquid stools, and often you have them many times a day, from 4 or 5 to 30. Because it is so uncomfortable and debilitating, the medical doctors and drug companies prey on your weakened state and offer you a drug or some potion to stop it. Do you really want to stop it?

Most all medical and drug treatments for diarrhea are to stop it. They are usually designed to stop your bowels natural peristalsis, the muscular contractions of your bowel. They are often referred to as bowel paralyzers. When taken, they stop the diarrhea by simply drugging and paralyzing your colon, so it can't eliminate. **This is very dangerous, and very typical of most medical and drug treatment that is usually designed to stop your body from doing what it is naturally trying to do, PROTECT YOU!** Literally stopping your body from protecting you and healing you. When you drug paralyze your bowel, well, of course the bacteria or other organisms love this, they multiply and you get worse, more poisoned that is, because your diarrhea is stopped. You may feel better for the moment, but as the bacteria grow, a relapse or a more lengthy recovery is certain. This is a very dangerous thing to do and can even be fatal.

NATURAL CURES FOR DIARRHEA

First, when having any digestive system problem, from gas, cramps, indigestion, heartburn, acid reflux, nausea all the way to diarrhea and EVERYTHING in between, always use my **Digestive Tonic**. 1 to 4 droppersful in an ounce of water will help your digestion back on its normal downward path, increase all digestive peristalsis, which in turn stops nausea, relaxes cramping and relieves all the symptoms I mentioned above. For diarrhea, use 4 to 8 droppersful in 2 to 4 ounces of water. So even with diarrhea, my **Digestive Tonic** is wonderful, especially with the gas, intestinal bloating, cramping and pain.

The absolute cure for diarrhea that does NOT go against what your body is trying to do, but actually aids and assists your body in many ways is my **Intestinal Formula #2**.

First and foremost the Activated Willow Charcoal in the formula, (this is why it is a bit black in color) absorbs and neutralizes any toxic bacteria and poison, encapsulates it and renders it harmless. This is why you will find charcoal in EVERY water filter manufactured. It absorbs over 3,000 known types of harmful bacteria, micro-organisms and other chemicals, toxin and poisons. If the charcoal in your water filter missed the bacteria, the charcoal in my Intestinal Formula #2 will get it. Having this in the formula starts absorbing what is giving you diarrhea the minute it reaches your bowel.

I also have Bentonite Clay in this formula that can absorb over 30 times its weight in toxic harmful substances and literally draws and vacuums this toxic material out of your bowel. It also contains Fruit Pectin, which removes other types of toxic material and residues.

These herbs absorb, neutralize and render harmless whatever you have been poisoned with *while* this material is still in your intestines. As a bonus, these herbs not only *neutralize* the poisons, but they also naturally coagulate your liquid stools so when they come out they are not liquid, but have a thicker consistency which is far more comfortable.

Second, the mucilaginous herbs like the Psyllium Seeds, Flax Seeds, Marshmallow Root, Slippery Elm Inner Bark and Fruit Pectin will also give you thicker more gelatinous, semi-formed and thicker consistency bowel movements, even though they may still be frequent until all the bacteria is gone. This is a pleasant rest from frequent brown water diarrhea discharges. Instead you will be having less frequent and *slightly formed* bowel movements, instead of watery discharges. Not only is this far more comfortable, but it can help you to avoid hemorrhoids as well. The mucilaginous herbs also soothe an inflamed, damaged, raw and bleeding intestinal lining and heal it fast.

Use one packet of the powder, or a heaping teaspoon of the bulk formula, at least 5 times or more a day, shaken in liquid as directed on the packet or the bulk jar, but you can use it every hour if necessary. Stop all food and fast until you are healed.

Also, I know you don't want to think about more pooping at a time like this, but often diarrhea is followed by constipation so have your **Intestinal Formula #1** or **Intestinal Formula #3** ready and waiting. Also, a few days after a bout of food poisoning or traveler's diarrhea is a perfect time to do my entire **5-Day BOWEL Detox**.

My friends, ~~shit~~ diarrhea happens. Everyone experiences it at some time in his or her life, whether you're a world traveler or just eat out occasionally at your local neighborhood grill.

The best way to avoid diarrhea is drinking clean water and eating clean food, especially when you are traveling. But also be prepared, and always have your **Intestinal Formula #2** on hand at home, in your car's glove box and anywhere you travel.

CHAPTER TEN
IS YOUR APPENDIX NECESSARY?

For your education I would like to set this issue straight.

Well, who am I to judge God and Nature. Obviously EVERYTHING in your body, every part, every organ, every cell is necessary, or it simply wouldn't be there. But we hear this time and time again, from some godless, ignorant medical doctor, *"this organ has no use"*, or *"this is a vestigial organ leftover from when we lived with dinosaurs and we don't need it anymore."* Well, if this theory of evolution was true, and we did live with dinosaurs, then wouldn't we have evolved, eliminated or grown out of any unnecessary organs and systems in our body?

If there is one organ of the human body I have heard more ignorant medical doctors make this statement about, more than any other, it is definitely the appendix. For your education,

and for theirs, I would like to set this issue straight.

Open any standard medical immune text and it will clearly tell you that the appendix is a lymphoid aggregation. Does this sound familiar? Yes, this is exactly the same as the tonsils. So you could call the appendix, "the tonsils of the bowel." As we know, any lymphoid aggregation, is a mass of lymph tissue, loaded with white blood cells, perfectly placed in an area to warn our immune system of invasion by bacteria, virus, fungus and other harmful micro-organisms, and is also the *military base* for immune cells to fight off any infection.

In fact, immunology textbooks also tell us that, once you get an appendectomy, the rest of your immune system doesn't work as well, especially the spleen. The spleen is a major component of our immune system, and one of the major reservoirs for our white blood cells. I quote from medical textbooks: *"The spleen's regeneration of lymphatic immune follicles and white blood cells after an attack by harmful micro-organisms, is **dependent on the presence of the appendix.**"* And, *"the spleen's potential to form antibodies is **also dependent on the presence of the appendix.** The appendix contributes to the recovery of the spleen's antibody-forming capacity by the production of antibody-forming cell precursors."*

When the appendix swells and is painful (exactly like the tonsils), it is telling us that there is an invasion of harmful bacteria, and our immune system is excreting white blood cells, and IS DEFENDING US! We wouldn't want to cut off our appendix any more than we would want to cut off our tonsils!

I could go on for hours about the pages and pages written about the function and necessity of the appendix in the maintenance of your health and having a functional strong immune system, but I believe I have made my point.

WHAT IS APPENDICITIS?

The appendix is right below your illeocecal valve (the entrance to the large intestine). Here is the perfect placement to detect any pathogen or micro-organism that may be harmful to you, as food enters the final stage of digestion before elimination. If the appendix detects anything harmful, it will get inflamed, much like your tonsils, and go on the offensive to kill the pathogen before it can be digested and circulate into your bloodstream. This is one of the ways you can get "appendicitis", and it's actually your body *protecting you*, not malfunctioning, as some medical experts will tell you.

The other, more common way you can get appendicitis is from backed-up fecal sludge in your large intestine. See, the appendix is located at the base of your ascending colon. This is the biggest anti-gravity and uphill trek for your digested food. Your appendix will actually excrete fluids to lubricate food and stimulate peristalsis (the muscular contractions of the colon that move everything along). But, if there are pounds of excess fecal matter sitting on top of your appendix, it can't do this very well. If your peristalsis is weak, then the feces just sits there festering, becoming toxic, until the appendix swells, gets sick, and, if left unattended long enough… BURSTS!

I've worked with a lot of people with appendicitis. I had one rule in my clinic. Nobody goes to the hospital. And, I had a second rule in my clinic. Nobody goes to the hospital. And, I had a third rule in my clinic. Nobody goes to the hospital.

Now that we've established this simple first rule we can go on to…

DR. SCHULZE'S APPENDICITIS REMEDY
STEP 1: STOP EATING NOW!

Don't put anything in your mouth. Don't. Stop eating immediately. You're already stuffed. You're so stuffed that poop is sitting on top of, and even inside of your appendix. So, stop eating.

STEP 2: GET THE GARBAGE OUT… FAST!

Get an enema. You've got to get that stuff out and give your appendix some relief. Natural Healing is very simple. It's always just a matter of STOPPING what is hurting you, and STARTING what will help you. So, if you're stuffed, and so much that your fecal matter is pushing into your appendix, stop stuffing and start eliminating. Dr. Christopher used to say that he gave so many enemas that one day he knocked on the door of one of his patients and they yelled, "Friend or enema?"

Basically, you want to get your bowel cleaned out quick. You want all the fecal matter out of that bowel, all the way up the descending colon, across the transverse, down the ascending, all the way to the cecum. You might even be able to get some of that fecal matter out of the appendix. It could take an hour or two working to get that bowel clean.

Once you've done your enema, you want to consume lots of

water and fresh juices. Start drowning yourself with fluid and flush your system. You might have a little fever too, so staying hydrated is important.

STEP 3: TAKE INTESTINAL FORMULA #1

90 Ct.

The next thing is to take **Intestinal Formula #1**. It'll take about 8 to 10 hours before you see the results of it, but take it anyway. Take it with some prune juice. Prune, yeah, any juice that will make you go. That would be the next thing to do.

Once the initial attack is over, I'd recommend doing my entire **5-Day BOWEL Detox** and also making some changes to your food program, but first things first.

STEP 4: DO SOME BODY WORK!

Now, you don't want to put your elbow right on the appendix and go for the gold, but you want to start some movement. The appendix is plugged up, so start some massage down at the iliac crest of the pelvis, and work your way up moving along the path of the large intestine. Also, get in the shower and do some hot and cold therapy right over the appendix where it hurts. This helps break up and move the congestion. Simply alternate with 15 seconds of hot water and 15 seconds of cold water for 7 repetitions (that's 7 hots and 7 colds).

FINAL THOUGHTS

These simple things always got my patients over their appendicitis. I've had calls where I wasn't able to be there, from all around the country, and I told people to do this exact routine and they got their children and their grandparents and everybody through their appendicitis. So it's not too difficult. And, I have never, ever seen or heard of anybody's appendix blowing up from doing this routine. They always got better. How soon? Three hours in some cases. Three days in others. It all depends on how sick you were. It depends on what you've been doing. Remember, the key is STOPPING what is making you sick and STARTING what will assist your body in healing itself.

CHAPTER ELEVEN
FREQUENTLY ASKED QUESTIONS

The following are the most commonly asked questions and concerns about bowel cleansing.

WHAT IS THE FOOD PROGRAM WHILE DOING YOUR 5-DAY BOWEL DETOX?

The reason for doing my **5-Day BOWEL Detox** in the first place is to first get your bowel to work better, more frequently, and more completely, to empty the waste out of your body. And secondly, it is to clean out old waste that has accumulated in your bowel.

The reason your bowel isn't working well and has accumulated waste is because of what you ate. Food that is difficult to digest and assimilate and food that is difficult to eliminate—processed foods, cooked foods, junk foods. So it only makes sense that when you're doing a bowel cleansing program, you wouldn't want to be consuming those foods that caused your bowel problem. So although you can eat a varied food program while you're doing the bowel cleanse, it would be nice to not be consuming the food that caused the bowel problem in the first place. Some people think they have to fast or just drink juices. That's not true. Other people would like to do the cleanse and not really modify their food program much. That's possible.

I would say for the average person, you can go ahead and consume food. But just make it so that during the **5-Day BOWEL Detox** that you're consuming clean food, the type of food that's loaded with fiber. Preferably a vegetarian diet. Fruits, vegetables, nuts, legumes, seeds and grains and sprouts. This type of food is loaded with fiber, loaded with nutrition, and it's not going to add to your bowel problem. In fact, it's going to aid the **5-Day BOWEL Detox** in scrubbing out your intestines. What you want to stay away from are refined flour products, like bread and pasta. Those things you could glue wallpaper to the wall with. And you want to stay away from animal products. Why? Because all animal products—beef, chicken, pork, fish, eggs, dairy—everything that had a face on it or came from anything with a face on it, has zero fiber. All this is going to do is slow down your bowel. All animal (fiber-less) food is going to do is cause further constipation and further plaquing in your bowel. So the main food program you would want to follow would be a clean vegetarian food program.

Now, if you want to assist the bowel cleanse or if you have had chronic problems with constipation or chronic problems with accumulated waste in your bowel, go ahead and assist it by making the food program even lighter. Have a few days of juice flushing in there. Go ahead and consume food for a day on your normal vegetarian, healthy, clean food program. Then, have a day or two of raw foods. Then, have a day of juice cleansing. Then go back to raw foods, and then go back to the vegetarian diet. That would assist your cleanse, and

certainly you can juice cleanse for the whole 5 days that you're doing this bowel program. But for the majority of people, just a clean, healthy, fiber-full vegetarian food program is the best way to eat while you're doing my **5-Day BOWEL DETOX.**

WHAT IF I AM AFRAID OF DOING THE PROGRAM?

For all of you out there who are afraid to start my **5-Day BOWEL Detox**, afraid you might not make it to the bathroom, don't be afraid. Your fear should be about going to a doctor. Your fear should be about ever having to go to a hospital. Believe me, the American Medical Association and the pharmaceutical industry have done a great job in brainwashing you if you're afraid to begin your own self-treatment, create a healthier lifestyle and use some herbs to heal yourself. That's exactly where they want you.

My job is to empower you. Come on, we're talking herbology and Natural Healing here. We're not talking about nuclear physics or advanced calculus. This is simple, and it's your God-given right to heal and cleanse and detoxify and build your strength and help yourself and your family members. So break free of that iron-clenching fist of the AMA and the drug companies that want you to be stupid and led like sheep to the slaughter in the hospital. Believe me, that's what they want.

I had thousands of patients in my practice, and believe me, I cleansed all their bowels, and they weren't a bunch of out-of-work bohemians. They all worked for a living. In fact, almost all of them were in the television and movie and music industry, and they couldn't just say, hey everybody, stop everything, I gotta go to the bathroom for about three hours. They worked regular jobs, they were regular people, and believe me, they all cleaned their bowels and they didn't have to take time off of work. Granted, when you're cleansing your bowels, you will notice that you have to go a lot more often. But it's not a big deal. It'll be very quick and complete. In fact, even if you go to the bathroom one extra time a day, I guarantee you, you'll be spending a lot less time in that bathroom. You can throw out all the magazines, because you won't have time to read anything. You'll sit down, you'll have your bowel movement, and you'll be out of there in two minutes flat. So don't use time as an excuse not to do the program.

WHAT IF I EXPERIENCE CRAMPING WHILE ON THE CLEANSE?

For those of you experiencing stomach cramps from taking the **Intestinal Formula #1**, relax. Any time you use a muscle that hasn't worked in a long time, you're going to feel it. This is no different than if you go to the gym for a week's worth of new workout sessions after years of a sedate lifestyle and no exercise. Believe me, you're going to feel it.

The analogy I always used with my patients in the clinic is, imagine you have an old car in the garage that maybe you inherited from your dad and you haven't started it up in a few years, and you decide one day to go out, charge the battery and crank it up. Is it going to run smooth at first? Of course not. It's going to shake, it's going to rattle, it's going to backfire from the carburetor and it's going to smoke from the exhaust. And then maybe in ten or fifteen minutes, it's going to smooth out and run nice.

So remember, when you first start taking the **Intestinal Formula #1**, you might have some cramping in your lower abdomen. You might feel it when you sit on the toilet the next day and that bowel starts to really work, the muscles contract, and you have a great bowel movement. That's great. You're alive. Remember, like that car, you might shake and sputter and skip and backfire and smoke and even stink a few minutes when you first start the bowel up, but I guarantee you, in a few weeks, in a month, that bowel is going to work and you're going to be absolutely thrilled you started working on healing and strengthening it.

I'VE TRIED OTHER COLON CLEANSES AND THEY DIDN'T WORK. HOW DO I KNOW YOURS IS GOING TO WORK?

In my clinic, I found that generally as patients came to me I'd say, "We're going to do some Herbal Therapy." They'd say, "I've tried herbs and they don't work." And, I used to get irritated by that. And then I went out and tried the majority of herbs, and I thought, they really don't work. And, it's not that the herbs don't work. I'm not blaming the herbal manufacturers, because they've just been beat up by the government for the last fifty years in America, but the idea became, don't make something that can cause any negative effects in anybody. Well, what that means is creating a product that won't cause any effect at all. So in

the clinic, I dealt with people differently. I figured we needed something strong. For some of my patients, I had to actually get out the old seventeenth and eighteenth century veterinarian books and come up with laxatives that were used for two thousand pound animals, like horses. That's the degree of constipation that we have in America today. I had patients that went once a month, and that wasn't unheard of. I had patients that went once every other month, a thirty-eight year old woman that went six times a year.

Then I had a record-breaker, a young lady from Northern California, who went only three times during her pregnancy, and then two times outside that, so we're talking five times a year. And my ultimate record-breaker was two bowel movements a year. So basically I concocted an emergency, full-strength formula that my brother originally named Depth Charges, because I gave it to him years ago and he said his bowel is still working great to this day. So don't worry about what any other herbal cleanses did or didn't do for you. Just trust me and try my **5-Day BOWEL Detox**.

HOW MANY TIMES SHOULD I DO YOUR 5-DAY BOWEL DETOX?

A lot of people wonder how many times they should do my **5-Day BOWEL Detox**. The answer is easy, and it applies to all cleansing. My patients, once they were well, once they were feeling great, with energy and vitality, and free of disease, I would suggest that they do one of my 5-Day Detoxes once every season. So, that's four times a year for a week. For most of my patients, I suggested my **5-Day BOWEL Detox** in the Spring, my **5-Day LIVER Detox** in the Summer, my **5-Day KIDNEY Detox** in the Fall and my **5-Day BOWEL Detox** again in the Winter.

SHOULD I DO THE 5-DAY BOWEL DETOX WHILE DOING EITHER THE 5-DAY LIVER DETOX OR 5-DAY KIDNEY DETOX?

A lot of people ask if they should be taking the **Intestinal Formula #1** and **#2** during the Liver and Kidney Flushes, and the answer is yes. Any time you're fasting, any time you're flushing, when you're doing your seasonal cleanse, any time you're cleaning yourself out, the foundation of any cleansing is the bowel program. You need to keep that bowel working and activated so that any debris that you're cleaning out of your body can get out immediately. Whatever program you're doing, make sure you're cleansing your bowel.

I saw many patients who had gone through many types of detoxification programs, and in the middle of those programs got themselves into deep trouble and came running to my clinic for help. And I was amazed at how many different so-called hip or sophisticated cleansing programs did not include getting the bowel working. I know some groups that put you in saunas and have you drink liquids, and that's great, that can really purge poisons out of your body, but if you haven't had a bowel movement in a week, you're going to be in a lot of trouble.

The foundation of any cleansing program or routine has to be getting that bowel working. In fact, it should have been working long before you even thought about another detoxification. Remember, in my clinic, I said you had to earn a cleanse by doing your homework up front.

CAN I STILL DO THE 5-DAY BOWEL DETOX IF I'M PREGNANT OR NURSING? AND IF I'M NURSING, IS IT HARMFUL TO THE BABY?

No, it is not harmful to the baby, and yes, you can do it while you're pregnant. In fact, you can do any of my programs. In extreme situations, where mom was going to die before delivering the child (in other words, maybe mom was given a month or two to live and the baby wasn't ready for five months) I even had moms do the **Incurables Program**, my thirty-day intensive cleansing and detox program, because mom was going to die and we were going to lose the baby. But in a normal situation, yes, mom can do any of these programs while she's pregnant. You just want to use your common sense. Certainly **SuperFood Plus** is the best for pregnancy and for nursing, because you're feeding either the fetus or that baby the best blood and then, once it's born, the best milk that you can imagine. Because you're fortifying your blood and your milk with **SuperFood Plus**.

The **Intestinal Formula #1**, well, here's where the common sense comes in. You shouldn't be sending yourself into an extensive, intensive, cathartic bowel movement in your eighth and a half month of pregnancy, unless you want to bring on labor. That said, you can use your **Intestinal Formula #1** even in your third trimester, that's no problem. Just don't cause some major bowel catharsis. Keep it simple and lower your dosage.

Once you have your baby, if you want to use your **Intestinal Formula #1**, that's fine. But remember, any herb you take will get through your milk into your baby on a reduced level. So you're also going to be treating your baby, too, which is great, because if your baby has an infection, you can take high dosages of **Echinacea Plus**, and it will get through the breast milk into your child. So yes, you can do all the programs when you're pregnant and when you're nursing. Just use your head and your good common sense.

CAN I TAKE INTESTINAL FORMULA #1 INDEFINITELY?

Most people start taking the **Intestinal Formula #1** and feel great. They love it. They're having regular, frequent, complete, full bowel movements, probably for the first time in their life. They feel great, they've lost weight, their tummy's flat, but then they wonder, can I take this formula for a while or a month or six months or a year, or even indefinitely? And of course, the answer is very simple. To poop or not to poop... that is the question.

The downsides of constipation are endless, are infinite. You can have sickness, illness, disease, immune weakness, low energy, back problems, headaches, leg pain, menstrual irregularity, hormone imbalance, emotional problems, bad digestion, poor assimilation... numerous diseases, including diverticulosis and herniation of the intestine due to impaction. Modern medicine says that a hundred percent of Americans, before they die, are going to have herniated intestines due to constipation. I saw hundreds of patients that developed cancer in the bowel simply because of constipation. I also saw every disease, every illness, no matter what it was, helped by cleaning out the bowel.

You may think that your disease or your problem is totally unrelated to your bowel, but let me tell you, the old Natural Healers knew it, and they were right. You clean out your bowel and miracles can happen. Now, for those whose diet and lifestyle inhibit them from having regular bowel movements, or those who have inherited sleepy and sluggish bowels, I couldn't suggest using this formula enough to get your regular bowel movements until the time comes when your bowel works perfectly on its own.

What's the downside? I don't know of any. Besides the cost of the herbs, there's none that I'm aware of. Rumors suggest that constant use of cathartic herbs will become addicting, but I've never, ever seen this. Constant use of cathartic herbs with no lifestyle change, well, if you want to continue to poop, you better keep taking the herbs. But on the other hand, I've seen thousands of people worldwide, including myself, that used **Intestinal Formula #1** for years and then, when their lifestyle was corrected and adjusted enough, the bowel started working naturally two to three times a day on its own. I'm one of those. I took the formula for over ten years before my lifestyle, my exercise program, my new emotional program and all of the good things I was doing kicked in enough for me to feel better and have those regular two to three bowel movements a day where my bowel moved thirty minutes after each major meal. So it can take some time, especially if you have years of hard living or bad living habits or, again, have inherited a very weak, sleepy bowel.

Once my patients would start having regular bowel movements without the formula, the only time they used **Intestinal Formula #1** again was during episodes of constipation, usually Thanksgiving, Christmas and any time the family gets together and eats, or when they traveled... any time they threw off their system and it resulted in constipation. Then you can use **Intestinal Formula #1** on a temporary basis, but believe me, my patients didn't get addicted.

I always say it's like going to the gym. If you do isolated biceps curls, that makes your biceps stronger, and when they're stronger they work better. So, so much for this rumor of addiction.

WHAT IS THE DOSAGE FOR INTESTINAL FORMULA #1?

Taking the **Intestinal Formula #1** is simple. Unless you want to learn the laws of jet propulsion, start with one capsule. It's a strong formula. The best way to take it is during or just after dinner. When you have some food in your stomach, take just one capsule. The next morning when you wake up, you might notice a dramatic difference in your bowel movements. If not, if you don't look at that toilet in amazement at what came out of you, then this evening with dinner take two capsules, and wait and see what happens the next day. You keep increasing by one capsule every day, and you'll know when you achieve the right dosage. You'll feel it. You'll feel that colon, that large muscle in your lower abdomen, beginning to work and removing all the bowel material.

I'VE ALREADY WORKED UP TO A HIGH NUMBER OF THE INTESTINAL FORMULA #1 AND I'M AFRAID TO TAKE MORE. WHAT DO I DO?

A lot of people with sluggish bowels work up to a high number of pills and are afraid to take any more. Don't be afraid. What we need to fear is all the health problems and diseases and illnesses that are caused by constipation.

There's no limit to the amount of **Intestinal Formula #1** you can take. I received a letter from one man in Hawaii who had to take 45 capsules before his bowel opened up. And after twenty-four hours of sitting on the toilet this man lost 52 pounds. That's right. 52 pounds of fecal matter! Now, this was a heavy man, well over 400 pounds. His wife was the one who told me this story, and she said to me, "You know, Dr. Schulze, I always knew he was full of crap." And she was right. As far as I know, 48 capsules is the record, and I doubt if it will take you that much. But don't be afraid to take as many capsules as you need to get your bowels working.

I'M HAVING TWO TO THREE BOWEL MOVEMENTS A DAY, BUT NOT THIRTY MINUTES AFTER EACH MEAL LIKE YOU SUGGEST. IS THIS OK?

Hey, remember, I'm going for perfection here. Like I said, when I examined primitive people who lived very natural lives, they would eat, and after every major meal, within about thirty minutes, their bowel would move. That's what I'd like to see, and that's the way most of my healthy

patients' bowels work most of the time. Not every time. Not everybody within thirty minutes evacuates their bowel. But that is a goal that you are going for. That is definitely a good goal, that at least one of your major meals that you eat during the day, whether in the morning, evening or midday, that thirty minutes afterward you have a bowel movement. That's when you know your bowel is getting really healthy and strong.

IF I'M HAVING A BOWEL MOVEMENT THIRTY MINUTES AFTER A MEAL, ISN'T THAT TOO FAST FOR ALL THIS FOOD TO BE MOVING IN AND OUT OF ME?

Well, not really, because the bowel movement that you're having thirty minutes after a meal is not the material from the meal that you just ate. Say you have a bowel movement thirty minutes after having your dinner. At best, that's your lunch. Probably, most likely, it's your breakfast. Maybe even the dinner from the night before. But it's not the food that you just ate coming out of you.

The reason is that when you start chewing food, you excrete saliva and you start out a peristalsis

ELIMINATION SCHEDULE

1. **Food enters stomach.**
2. **Peristalsis triggers the small intestines.**
3. **Previous meal exits.**

action, a muscular wave in your esophagus that works its way down to your stomach that also squeezes to help digest the food that you're eating. But at the same time, a peristalsis is triggered in your small intestine. There's a triggering reaction, and that starts helping you digest, assimilate and eliminate the meal that you ate before. And that usually starts a wave going of peristalsis or muscular movement, contraction and action in your colon which will start you to eliminate the previous meal or two meals after you eat your current meal. So what am I saying? When you have a meal and a bowel movement thirty minutes later, you are not excreting the food that you just ate. It's from one or two, if not three, meals ago.

I'M EXPERIENCING A LOT MORE GAS WHEN I USE YOUR INTESTINAL FORMULA #1. IS THAT OK, OR AM I ALLERGIC?

Well, no, you're not allergic, and that's perfectly OK. I always use the analogy, if you had an old car in your garage and you hadn't started it in years and you went out and started cranking the engine you might get explosions out of the carburetor or backfires

out of the rear end, and it would shake and sputter, but after about fifteen minutes it's going to hum, it's going to run well. Well, this is just like your bowel. When you have more gas it means that the **Intestinal Formula #1** is breaking up old deposits of fecal matter, stuff that's in there for years, the fudgsicle you ate when you were fourteen, all those candy bars you had on Halloween when you were five. Let me tell you, there's a lot of old material in everybody's bowel, and the

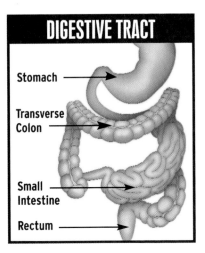

DIGESTIVE TRACT

Stomach

Transverse Colon

Small Intestine

Rectum

Intestinal Formula #1 breaks up that old fecal matter, that old toxic poisonous material. And when it does that, you can often get a little more gas.

If you want to help relieve the gas, use my **Digestive Tonic** along with the **Intestinal Formula #1**, and that will give you more gas-relieving capability. Take a couple droppersful in about an ounce of water, knock it back, and that will help move the gas on.

WHY CAN'T I CONTINUE HAVING REGULAR BOWEL MOVEMENTS WHEN I STOP TAKING THE INTESTINAL FORMULA #1?

Well, there's a couple reasons for this. One is your bowel is not healed and strong enough yet. Remember, taking **Intestinal Formula #1** is like sending your colon to the gym and doing an isolated biceps curl. Every time you take that formula it works the muscles of your bowel, creating more peristalsis. So every time you take that formula, your bowel gets cleaner and stronger. But, it doesn't happen overnight. Some people need to take the formula for months, others for up to a year.

Personally, I had to take that formula for twelve years before my bowel (because I inherited a very bad bowel) worked perfectly on its own. And now, I only take the formula maybe once or twice a year, maybe if I'm traveling (because that can cause constipation), or if I go to too many parties in a row, have some food that really isn't on my day-

to-day program and want to get it out of my body. But that's the main reason.

Also, another reason is maybe your lifestyle, especially your food program, hasn't changed enough yet, or you haven't had those changes made for a long enough period. Because, remember; so many things also affect your peristalsis, like the type of food you're eating. Is it live enough? Is it raw enough? Does it have enough fiber? Does it have enough enzymes? The more you get towards that good, organic fruit, vegetable, vegan food program, the better your bowel is going to work.

Also, lifestyle changes. If you're happy, your bowel is going to work much better than if you're unhappy. Maybe you sit in an office all day long, and that certainly isn't going to promote the bowel to move as much as it would if you were working outside and up and moving.

So, again, the two reasons that when you stop the **5-Day BOWEL Detox** that your bowel stops working is, one, your bowel isn't strong enough yet, so continue the program, and two, your food program and your lifestyle changes need to be more dramatic or need to be better for a longer period of time. So don't stop them, either. In fact, make your food program cleaner, get in more exercise and make your lifestyle changes, keep up with your **Intestinal Formula #1**, and you, like all my patients, will end up having a perfect bowel.

CAN I START TAKING THE INTESTINAL FORMULA #2 RIGHT AWAY?

Capsules

Do not start taking the **Intestinal Formula #2** until you get your bowels working. I suggest, in all the literature, that you use the **Intestinal Formula #1** for a week

and then, as your bowels are regulated, you start with the **#2**. But do not start the **Intestinal Formula #2** until your bowels are regulated. So for those of you who are constipated or who have had years of constipation or maybe have inherently weak bowels, don't be in any hurry. Nobody should be in any hurry to start **Intestinal Formula #2**. Stay on **Intestinal Formula #1** until you are having regular, frequent bowel movements that put a smile on your face every morning, and you're starting to

have bowel movements even at other times during the day after your meals. And when you're feeling really good about your bowel and the way it's working, then you start the **Intestinal Formula #2**.

WHY DOES INTESTINAL FORMULA #2 CONSTIPATE ME?

Some people take the **Intestinal Formula #2** and find that it constipates them, and there's a few reasons for this. First off, remember, the whole time you're using the **Intestinal Formula #2** you should also be using the **Intestinal Formula #1**. In fact, if you read the directions you should be using more of it than you normally need, because **Intestinal Formula #2** is the great drawing, cleansing, detoxifying formula for the bowel. It's going to go in there and pull out everything. But on its own, inherently, **Intestinal Formula #2** is constipating for most people, especially if you suffer from some form of constipation. So if you just take **Intestinal Formula #2** on its own, it may just solidify your bowels and stop them from working.

The first step is getting a good dosage of **Intestinal Formula #1** down, to where your bowels are working and you're very happy with the frequency and completeness of your bowel movements, and then increase it by a capsule or maybe even two, and then begin the week-long process of **Intestinal Formula #2**.

DO I HAVE TO CONSUME THE WHOLE BOTTLE OR BOX OF PACKETS OF INTESTINAL FORMULA #2?

Yes. **Intestinal Formula #2** is designed for one person to consume in one week, and it's not until you finish the bottle that you finish the cleanse. If you are using **Intestinal Formula #2** capsules, your goal is to take 10 capsules 5 times per day for the next 5 days. That is 50 capsules a day. If you are using **Intestinal Formula #2** packets, then simply take 5 packets 5 times a day for the next 5 days. Remember, during this program on average you will be taking **Intestinal Formula #2** (capsules or packets) every 2 to 3 hours throughout the day.

I'M TAKING YOUR INTESTINAL FORMULA #2, BUT ISN'T THIS BLACK DRINK A BIT RADICAL?

Well, let me tell you something. It doesn't taste black, and it doesn't taste radical. Some people are so brainwashed by modern medicine that they begin to think that herbal medicine and Natural Healing is radical. They think that medical doctors and the practice of modern medicine is normal, is rational, but that herbs and Natural Healing is radical. People who think this are the living proof of the success of one of the greatest con jobs in American history. And this con job is to sell medicine to a society of people, but scare them out of ever taking their healing into their own hands. Let me tell you something, kidney dialysis, that's radical. That should be in a vampire movie. Liver and heart transplants, that's radical.

The fact that even medical universities like Stanford, say that the human body should live a hundred and twenty-five years but we're all dying in our early seventies... that's radical. Let me tell you radical.

I had a patient who was in her early thirties, and she had an aggressively growing brain tumor. The doctors did a surgery, and they opened up her skull and they scooped most of the tumor out, but they couldn't get it all. They closed her back up, where she laid in intensive care for almost thirty days. She said she was in the worst pain of her entire life. She was totally paralyzed, couldn't talk, couldn't communicate, couldn't even blink her eyes, and she said it felt like someone had hot nails driving through her head, and every moment of every day, every second, she was screaming silently to herself. That's radical.

Let me tell you, I had a patient who had a tumor in her rectum, and the doctor said, "Hey, let us do some pinpoint, laser-guided smart bomb radiation treatment and we'll get rid of that tumor." I tried to explain to her that radiation treatment is not that smart and not that well-guided and that she could end up with a horrible burn and that we should try Natural Healing. But no, she went ahead and had her radiation treatment on that tumor, and two days later when she was having a bowel movement, the bowel material came out her vagina, because they burned out the wall between her rectum and her vagina. Friends, that's radical. Get with it here.

There is nothing radical about going out into your backyard and finding a few plants that God has provided for our food and for our medicine. This is not radical. Natural Healing and water treatments and exercise and

being happy and having a great spiritual life, this is not radical. Mutilating surgery, burning toxic radiation and killer chemicals called chemotherapy, this is radical. **Intestinal Formula #2** has a little charcoal, a little fruit pectin and a few herbs. This formula may be black in color, but mix it with juice, it will taste just fine, it will clear years of poisons out of your bowel, and I assure you, it is nowhere near a radical treatment.

IF I HAVE CROHN'S DISEASE OR COLITIS OR IRRITABLE BOWEL SYNDROME, HOW DO I APPROACH THE CLEANSE?

For those of you with Crohn's disease or colitis or irritable bowel syndrome, do not start with the **Intestinal Formula #1. Intestinal Formula #1** is for about 98% of the people out there, the people with sluggish bowels, maybe a history of constipation, but who do not have a bowel movement twenty to thirty minutes after each major meal.

The other 2%, those who are having too many bowel movements, don't need to increase their bowel movements, and that's what the **Intestinal Formula #1** does. So instead of using the **Intestinal Formula #1**, just go right to the **Intestinal Formula #2**. If you're one of those two percent, you'll love it. You'll think it puts the fire out in your bowel. It'll soothe the irritated tissue, reduce the inflammation in your colon, and solidify the diarrhea-like bowel movements. You'll feel wonderful. Believe me, it will be a blessing in your life to start on the **Intestinal Formula #2**.

Organic Garlic

IS IT CONSTIPATION THAT CAUSES A FECAL ENCASEMENT?

Yes. Basically, as Americans, we're not big on fiber. We love meat, dairy, chicken, fish, eggs, cheese, and the first thing people have to realize is, animal equals zero fiber. Anything that came from an animal has no fiber, which means it sits in your bowel, and it really won't go anywhere until you consume something that has fiber, which pushes it out. So the good old American food program of bacon and eggs is literally stuck down there.

I had patients that during a bowel cleanse, after having already done three or four previous cleanses, would eliminate the entire casing of the inside of their bowel. I'm talking five feet long here, and they'd eliminate it in one bowel movement. And they'd be frightened, because they thought they were losing their

colon, not just eliminating the old toxic liner. And you could even see the sacks on it; they would come out at the same time. But during normal bowel cleansing, those diverticuli don't get emptied. It takes a little bit of advanced bowel cleansing to get rid of them.

DO I NEED TO BE TAKING ACIDOPHILUS?

For those of you worried about taking acidophilus or lacto-bacillus bacteria after doing the bowel cleanse, I ask you this: Who said that my program took the flora out of your bowel? If you're on a good food program with some nice raw fruits, vegetables, sprouts, soaked beans and all those good things, you shouldn't have any problem with your intestinal flora. And if you think you do, think about fermented veggies and garlic.

Garlic is wonderful for your intestinal flora, and raw sauerkraut and Anne Wigmore's Rejuvelac, and fermented soy yogurts and seed cheeses, and all those wonderful things that you can use to get bacteria back in your bowel.

And if you're really worried or have a history of problems, then sure, you can take some bacteria, like various lacto-bacillus strains, but when you do, please stay away from the ones that are made with dairy products. Use the ones—I see them all the time—that are made with apple juice and other great foods instead of getting near all that cow juice that's just going to constipate you and cause problems all over again. And now that you've cleaned out your bowel, you don't want that. But if you need to, or if you feel you need to, sure, you can take some added bacteria to help your intestinal flora.

ARE THERE THINGS YOU EAT THAT ACTUALLY STAY IN YOUR COLON FOR YEARS AND YEARS?

Yes. It's actually a medical fact more than a Natural Healing fact. The Merck Manual is the American standard, if not the international standard, of diagnoses of disease. It's produced by Merck Research Laboratories, one of the largest drug companies in America, and it's a standard medical text of disease used around the world. Every doctor has one. And their

statistics say that in 1950, 10% of all Americans had diverticulosis, or herniated sacs, in their colon caused by the pressure and stuffing of constipation, where fecal matter literally pushes into a weak part, or a balloon, in the wall of the muscle of the bowel and stays there. But in 1955, they raised that to 15%. And in 1972, they went up to 30%, and in the 1987 edition, they said just about half of Americans have diverticulosis or herniated sacs in their colon. And in the most recent edition of the Merck Manual, it says if people live long enough, every American will have herniated bowel pockets or diverticuli (which are just like a weak spot on a balloon or a rubber tire where it bulges), and they get filled with fecal matter. And basic common sense will tell you it just stays in there. In fact, the whole colon can get encased in fecal matter in advanced constipation, to where it looks like a rusty pipe, an old steel or galvanized pipe in your house, and when you look through it you can only see a small hole.

HOW CAN AN HERB STIMULATE A SLUGGISH BOWEL THAT'S BEEN A CHRONIC PROBLEM?

It's great. I'm always amazed by how many people say, I don't get it, how do herbs work? And I think, I don't get it, how do they not? We don't question food, do we?

All food, herbs, plants, trees, barks, berries, resins, strawberries and blueberries and anything that grows on this planet contain chemicals. Some of these chemicals are nutritional, like vitamins, minerals and enzymes. Other chemicals are stronger, like essential oils and alkaloids, and they're very medicinal. All the original classic prescription drugs in America were isolated from chemicals found in plants.

Over 50% of the drugs used today were originally chemicals found in herbs. Herbs simply work off chemicals. There's a group of chemicals called anthroquinones, and there's a particular anthroquinone, called Emodin, which is in certain herbs like the aloes that grow equatorially around the world, or Senna Pods and Leaves, which were famous throughout recorded history as laxatives even in ancient Egypt.

And then there's Cascara Sagrada, which is our California plant. These all contain the Anthroquinone Emodin, and Emodin, when it gets inside your bowel and touches your colon wall, actually makes the muscle move. It stimulates that muscle to move. It's kind of like going to the gym. You're strengthening that muscle by stimulating it to move. And it stimulates it to move so much that in one naturopathic school we took a bowel out of a dead person and when we smeared the different Emodin herbs in it, the bowel actually contracted. So hence comes my statement that I've been accused of making a few times, that I can even get a dead person to have a bowel movement. And it comes from the fact that I don't need any participation from the patient.

These herbs are powerful enough to make the bowel contract and work. It starts that muscular peristalsis, specifically in the colon. So it's going to make your bowel work tomorrow, and I don't care what you're eating, drinking or thinking. We'll get right, but that might take a month or two. Right now, tomorrow, I need your bowel to work. So I made the **Intestinal Formula #1** in the clinic to guarantee me that I could get my patients' bowels to work regardless of whether or not they had corrected anything yet. I had to get the elimination channels, the channels of waste removal, working in the body and the herbs are what did it.

"In my Natural Healing books, videos, CDs, DVDs and audiotapes, I teach you how life-threatening diseases, a growing epidemic in America, are so easy to prevent and so simple to heal NATURALLY with my powefully effective programs."
— *Dr. Richard Schulze*

CHAPTER TWELVE
ADDITIONAL RESOURCES

Get Well: How To Create Powerful Health

▸ Let Dr. Schulze introduce you to his philosophies of Natural Healing

▸ Learn the importance of attitude, emotions and spirituality in the quest for health

▸ Listen to stories from Dr. Schulze's clinic

▸ Learn Dr. Schulze's 20 simple and easy steps toward a healthy new life

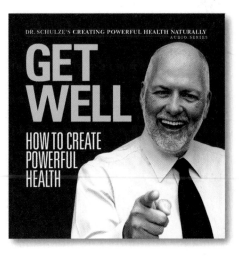

Ask for your FREE copy today!
Call 1-800-HERB-DOC (437-2362)
or visit us at WWW.HERBDOC.COM

DR. SCHULZE'S
HERBAL PRODUCT CATALOG

Dr. Schulze's Catalog Includes...

- ▸ **Easy to understand descriptions of ALL his powerfully effective Herbal Formulae**

- ▸ **His common sense Natural Healing Wisdom and Clinical Experiences**

- ▸ **NEW Herbal Formulae and Clinical Detox Programs**

- ▸ **Plus many new inspiring Customer Testimonials and Healing Miracles**

Dr. Schulze's 8 Clinical Herbal Formulae For Digestion & Elimination

On This DVD:

▸ **Constipation Record Breakers**

▸ **Medical Statistics On Bowel Disease**

▸ **What is a Normal Bowel Movement?**

▸ **6 Natural and Healthy Ways To Get Your Bowel Working Better**

▸ **Dr. Schulze's 8 Clinical Herbal Formulae for Digestion and Elimination**

...and more!

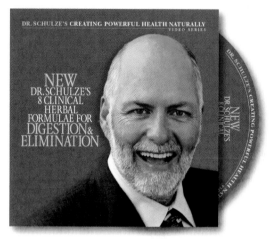

Ask for your FREE copy today!
Call 1-800-HERB-DOC (437-2362)
or visit us at WWW.HERBDOC.COM